PROOF COPY
NOT FOR
RESALE

Finding
LOST

Nancy Lafleur

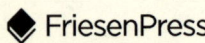 FriesenPress

Suite 300 - 990 Fort St
Victoria, BC, V8V 3K2
Canada

www.friesenpress.com

Copyright © 2017 by Nancy Lafleur
First Edition — 2017

All rights reserved.

No part of this publication may be reproduced in any form, or by any means, electronic or mechanical, including photocopying, recording, or any information browsing, storage, or retrieval system, without permission in writing from FriesenPress.

ISBN
978-1-5255-1213-1 (Hardcover)
978-1-5255-1214-8 (Paperback)
978-1-5255-1215-5 (eBook)

1. BIOGRAPHY & AUTOBIOGRAPHY, NATIVE AMERICANS

Distributed to the trade by The Ingram Book Company

Finding LOST

CHRISTMAS DINNER

The shoppers were everywhere. Some were rude and annoying, but a few would flick her a loonie or any other spare change they may have had. "Christmas, what for?" she yelled in her mind. Everywhere she walked, there were reminders of what she never had. In every corner of the mall, she could faintly hear bells ringing, men standing here and there with their Santa hats collecting money for the poor. Anna didn't go into the mall very much anymore, instead she stood close to entranceways waiting for the next generous soul to spare her a dime. It was a dark pitted routine she fell into, but didn't know how to escape. She knew a good stiff drink would make it all go away, and so she stood there begging for what she needed just to survive today.

Anna had left home at the exhausted age of fourteen. She left her small town life behind, trading it in for the larger city that was only a few hours away. She often thought of going back, but it seemed a million miles away. The day she left, she had hitched a ride with the local bootlegger; she hopped in the back of his truck and watched her home fade into a memory as they drove south.

She was almost fifty now, but she felt a hundred. Sometimes she wondered why the good Lord even kept her alive. Thirty-five years of this hell was enough, and sometimes she just wanted it to end. Waking up each morning was as painful as falling asleep. It was all a part of her routine now. Wake up, head downtown, find some money, buy a bottle, drink, and then find a place to sleep. Sometimes her routine would change if she couldn't collect enough money to buy her bottle of "escape" or "forget." It was these days she would head to the local women's shelter for a hot shower, change of clothes, hot meal, and hopefully a bed to sleep in. She called these vacation days.

Today was a "good" day. She had already mustered up five dollars. It was that "spirit of giving," that was to her advantage. People seemed friendlier this time of year, although there were always the jerks. She would convince herself, that she was stronger than they were; she could out-survive those bastards on these streets. "These jerks wouldn't last the night," she would mutter to herself each time she was insulted or told to get lost. She was cold, hungry, and needed to find warmth. She knew this city; she knew where to find the warm air vents that worked better than an outdoor campfire. She huddled in the alleyway of the mall, close to the vents of the food court. The warm air vent blew down on her, keeping her warm, but also dousing her with the scent of food. The scent took her back... She reminisced about the smell of her grandmother's cooking. Her mind fell into a dream state. Leaning up against the cold brick wall, she closed her eyes. As warm air blew on her body, she fell back in time.

The smell of the turkey woke her from her sleep. Her grandmother had already been up for hours preparing the turkey they would have for dinner that day. At the age of four, there were no real expectations of Christmas. If she didn't see other people's traditions, how would she know anyway? All she understood was there was going to be a meal that did not consist of rabbit. It had been a very cold night in the cabin, and the warmth of the woodstove was pleasant.

She was tired. It was quiet in the cabin, except for the wind blowing against the plastic on the covered windows. The silence meant that either her grandfather had made it home and had fallen asleep, or he hadn't made it home yet. At an early age, she knew too well what this meant. Her grandparents had been drinking the night before; the usual fight broke out and the usual beating on her grandmother happened. At this early age, her only defence was to find a place to hide, afraid she too would be hit. She would cry in fear until the beating ended, afraid she might find her grandmother dead.

The fighting always seemed to last forever; her grandfather would swear at her grandmother, saying things no child should ever hear. He would accuse her of sleeping with other men, and then would throw things at her. From under the covers, she could hear the fists hitting up against her grandmother's face. Her grandmother would scream for help, but there was no one. No one was near, and no one was coming.

Then it would be all over, in the midst of the night, she would stay covered and listen to the sobs of her grandmother. Her grandfather would either go to bed or leave after he had beaten his wife. This time he had left, and when it was all over, she could hear the cabin door close. It was only when the coast was clear, she would peek out from under her covers, praying her grandmother was all right. This time, she found her with blood all over her face. To help her grandmother, she took a cloth and tried her best to wipe the tears and blood that now masked her face. Her grandmother would crawl into bed, and in the darkness of the night, she could hear her sobs.

"Got a drink, Sista?" the voice startled her back to reality.

"NO!" she hollered back.

"Holy, settle down!" the reply came back.

It was Sheila, her sister. Well at least out here, they called one another friends or by family kinship. Sheila was not her blood sister, but she was the closest thing to being one. Sheila was a feisty woman, and this is why she hung around her. No one messed with you if you were with Sheila. She was not large, but her rough looking man features told you she was tough. Her hair was all white, but this did not fool anyone into thinking she was a gentle old lady. She had a mouth that would make a miner blush. Her hands were rough, and told stories of takedowns, and booze hugging. Sheila was by no means easy on the eyes, but her soul was gentle once you got to know her. She too had a story like everyone on these streets. Sheila shuffled around the corner to where Anna was standing, to try warming up a little from the winter cold. Together they stood huddled to share a quick cigarette butt that Anna had found earlier.

Sheila was down and out, so today it was Anna's turn to look after her. Something family would do. Anna had family. Somewhere. She was not proud to be the eldest in her family. She should have been the one to lead by example, but instead she ran away. In her mind, she never stopped running.

FINDING LOST   7

She told Sheila she would catch up with her later, and just maybe she would have enough money to buy them a bottle of Christmas cheer. At that moment, she just wanted to be alone. She was tired, tired of the cold, tired of drinking her sorrows away. Tired of living. Today her mind was tired too. In fact, it was stuck on replay, and each time she closed her eyes she was back at the cabin where she grew up for some years. Anna found a wooden crate nearby. She pulled up against the wall and used it as a make shift chair. She sat, took a deep breath, and closed her eyes to rest. She went back into her daydream state and once again started to remember.

She went back to her place in Molanosa, that Christmas morning. She slipped quickly back to that nice smell of turkey, cooking.

She remembered crawling out of her blankets and looking towards the kitchen table. Her grandmother was sitting there, her head turned toward the window. She was sipping on a cup of tea. As she began to make her presence known in the room, her grandmother slowly turned her face toward her. Suddenly, just like that, someone switched a light switch and her memory moved into an old black and white movie; it was all in slow motion and there was no volume. Anna touched her cheeks; she felt the warm tears rolling down. She would never forget that face. Her grandfather had beaten her grandmother so bad her face was swollen; so swollen it was almost beyond recognition. There was a huge gash above her eyebrow, and she couldn't open one eye. Her nostrils were plugged with blood that had dried. Anna's tears started running faster as she reflected on the sacrifices this woman made just to try make Christmas a little bit memorable for her.

Anna snapped herself back to reality. After all these years, she remembered it like it was yesterday. The pain too, was still real. She looked around the alleyway hoping to see someone, so she could bum a smoke, but it was quiet. Anna felt warmer now, and decided to move on from the alley. She decided to make her way to the park where she may run into Sheila. She wasn't sure where the day would take her, but for some reason, she didn't really care. She thought sitting at her usual bench might give her some perspective. She was tired, her legs were tired, and her whole body ached too. Anna felt everything about her was tired, and maybe even broken beyond repair.

As she walked to the park, she moved slowly, making a fresh trail after a morning snowfall. The wind was blowing, and the cold quickly found its way into her bones. Her jacket was not made for those conditions and, she knew in time, she would have to walk across town to the Salvation Army for a warmer one. "Not today" she thought, "Maybe tomorrow." Today, she had no energy for the long ten-block trek. Instead, Anna found her usual bench in the park and proceeded to clean the snow off. As she is dusted off the snow with her coat sleeve, she spotted a group of women walking towards her. They were each carrying large white bags filled with Christmas shopping, Anna speculated. They were laughing. At her? She wondered. She sat on her bench waiting for them to pass, but they didn't. Instead, they stopped right in front of her and one of them asked her if she wanted like a blanket. "Wow! Christmas for Anna! What the hell, sure I will take one," she told the lady. And as quick as she was gruff, she minded her manners, and added, "Thank you." The ladies all smiled and continued walking. From her bench, Anna watched them as they walked away, laughing as if they were programmed robots. Anna sat holding the plaid fleece blanket on her lap. "Not the largest, or the warmest blanket," she thought, "but it's better than nothing." And nothing was all she had right now. "A small blanket to help with the cold, this bench to myself, memories of past… so this is what it comes down to," Anna thought as she pulled the blanket closer and closed her eyes to rest.

As quick as she closed her eyes, she returned to that look on her grandmother's face, but this time no tears came. Instead, she felt anger for the man that would harm such a gentle soul. "What a bastard," she whispered to herself. "What a bastard!" The rest of that Christmas morning had some memories missing, but one thing for sure, there were no Christmas gifts or even a tree. Her grandfather had thrown that out days before already, during another drunken stupor. Somewhere during that morning, her grandfather returned to the cabin, to the site of the brutal beating he had laid on his wife just hours before. She remembered him sitting at the kitchen table in their tiny cabin, barking orders for eggs and tea. Her grandmother cooked the eggs, and Anna helped by pouring the tea. At the age of four, she too, knew how to walk on eggshells. After her grandfather ate, he went to bed, leaving them at peace for the time being.

Peace. Quietness. Anna loved it! Peace was always temporary, never a forever thing. "I will find the best peace when I die," Anna told herself, giving herself something to look forward to, but for that day, she would find peace in the cold and with her new blanket. The rest of her morning was spent thinking of what was, what happened, and questions to God on why he hated her so much. Of course, at times, she had convinced herself there was no God. A good God would never allow people to suffer the way she had, and the way her grandmother had. She hated life most days. She hated seeing what others had, and knew that she would never enjoy even a morsel of it.

Anna forced herself to snap out of her dream. She heared a vehicle stop nearby, and listened to a door closing. She opened her eyes and recognized the red jacket. It was Cheryl. Anna liked Cheryl; she had always treated Anna well and with respect. Cheryl was no stranger to street walking and had spent a few years in Edmonton as a prostitute. Cheryl gave up her crazy life after this one time she was beaten so badly she almost couldn't walk again. Cheryl found God, moved back home, became educated, and was now someone Anna called "friend."

Anna didn't move from her spot, and remained seated on her bench. She reached up to take the coffee Cheryl handed her. Cheryl sat with Anna for a little while and they talked. Cheryl told Anna she had others to go see, but reminded her that God was always with her. She thanked Cheryl for the coffee and teased her by saying, "God quit liking me a few years back." She chuckled and Cheryl reached over to give her a small, but meaningful hug. As Cheryl got up to leave, she also reminded Anna of the detox centers she could check herself into. Anna laughed and said, "What you talking about? I've been sober for eighteen hours now," and laughed. Cheryl waved good-bye and drove off.

The snow started to come down again, but it was light. The snowflakes were large; Anna looked up into the sky, and allowed them to fall on her face. They were cold, but refreshing. The snowflakes cleansed the tears that had fallen early that morning, and Anna started to think again. She wondered why she was dealt this hand. Did she have a choice? She closed her eyes, and again feels the tears starting to warm her face. She couldn't seem to leave that day behind, her first memory of Christmas.

Anna remembered spending the rest of that Christmas morning sitting quietly at the table, afraid to make a noise. She wanted her grandfather to wake up sober, so they could have a nice turkey dinner. Her grandmother was on the other side of the cabin, her back toward Anna. She avoided facing

Anna, not so much out of embarrassment, but more so to save Anna the pain of seeing her this way again. There was silence in the little cabin, but fear was hovering like a big, thick cloud. Anna wanted this day to be good. She thought about the turkey in the oven. Her grandmother tended to it now and again, ensuring there was enough wood burning in the big white stove. Every so often, her grandmother opened the lid of the roaster, allowing the aroma to escape the pan. The aroma filled the cabin quickly, and each time, Anna imagined a meal that will fill her empty stomach.

Anna awakened to another aroma, the smell of hot soup. She had not left her bench, but her site had become a busy place for outreach workers. This time it was Ken from the church group, handing her a cup of soup. "Are you all right, Anna?" he asked her.

"Why the hell you care?" she squawked at him.

"Okay, okay, just checking in on you. I love you too Anna, have a nice day." He chuckled, and then left.

Left alone on her bench, Anna decided to sit and sip on her hot cup of soup. It had been a while since she had something to eat, and she was actually thankful to Ken, although she would not tell him that. The cup of soup was filling and it gave her the energy she needed to move on. For some strange reason, Anna really didn't want to drink today. She just wanted to be alone, in her thoughts, and in her own space. Anna decided to move down to the riverbank.

As a child, she lived close to the creek, and that sound of moving water always took her to another place, not this earth, but to a better and more peaceful place. Today, she yearned to be there. The water of the river was still moving, and for most winters, it did not freeze completely. Anna decided to head to the monument by the river. A few years back, there had been some type of "monument" built for some white guy who was some type of hero. Apparently, he would bring supplies through the river route during the fur trade. Anna was quick to criticize and think they probably hauled in kids for the Residential School that once sat just a mile up the way. "Don't see a monument for that!" Anna thought to herself. Anna spotted the monument and made her way to the nice gazebo just to the left of it. She stood there for a while before going down to the riverbank. There was some ice forming on the edges that had caught Anna's attention. She left her blanket on the bench of the gazebo and took her time walking down. Anna stopped short of the river's edge, and sat on the bench nearby. She closed her eyes and pointed her head up toward the skies.

She returned to the cabin that had been playing in her mind all day, and begins at the place she had left off from moments ago. She was back in the cabin, smelling that incredible turkey, that she would soon eat, along with other things her grandmother had been working on. Potatoes, gravy, stuffing, and homemade cranberry sauce from the cranberries she and her grandmother had picked earlier that fall. She remembered her grandmother setting the table for three. It would be just the three of them. No one would be joining them that day, nor would they be joining any other families either. Her memory stopped for a second, and this time the tears were flowing as if someone had just destroyed a beaver dam. Her memory moved quickly to that moment her grandfather woke up in a rage. There was nothing now to hold it back, him getting up, and swearing at her grandmother just as she was taking the turkey out of the oven. She remembered him grabbing the whole roaster with his bare hands, and heaving it out the door. She screamed in fear, and ran out the door crying. No shoes, no jacket, she ran past the turkey that was now laying in the snow, as steam came up from the heat hitting the cold, cold snow. The roaster cover was lying to its side, halfway in the snow; the other half was completely upside down. Her grandmother was behind her, telling her to run to her Aunt Martha's house, which was through a path a short distance away. As she ran, the smell of the turkey left her nostrils and she was suddenly not hungry anymore.

As her memory faded of another Christmas ruined, Anna knew that one day she would have to bury this memory for the last time. It was her ghost. Unfortunately, that ghost had nothing to give, but at this point, she wanted nothing but peace. She ached for that kind of peace, the kind that lasted a lifetime, not just on snowy cold days like the one today.

Anna got up from the bench and very slowly made her way to the riverbank. There was no one around, just her, the sky, and the water below. She could hear the water moving. It was quiet and she liked this sound. As she got closer to the edge, she saw how the ice had formed on the riverbank. It was about a foot into the river and appeared solid. As a child, Anna remembered playing on these, hoping they would not crack and sweep her into the flowing waters. She looked at the ice and once again dared herself to step on it. Her only wish this time was maybe the ice would crack. Very slowly, Anna put one foot on the ice, and told herself, "Just one foot," she said, "just one foot."

MEET ME IN THE MOONLIT SKY

"Grandma, I'm scared," were Jasmine's first thoughts when she finally became conscious. She had no clue where she was. She was guessing that maybe she was alive, but was really not sure. She thought maybe this was death and that she had ended up in hell. She knew she'd end up there anyway, so maybe this really was the end. "Oh my God, I am dead!" she screamed in her mind. She was confused, and unable to talk. She tried to move her mouth but was unable to spit out any words. Her lips seemed as though someone had taken crazy glue and glued them shut.

She felt parts of her body, but for other parts, she felt nothing. Her head felt like a bowling ball. It was heavy, and she could not lift it. She felt warmth on her body, her skin was exposed, and guessed that maybe she was naked. She tried hard to open her eyes, but they too felt tight and as if someone had glued them as well. She tried to yell, maybe holler for some help but there was something in her throat preventing her from screaming.

Her limbs felt attached, but attempting to move them was painful. It was within this moment of consciousness she became very afraid. She wanted life, wanted to live. She did not want to die, without really having lived. She had thoughts of her two children finding her, although she knew that would never happen. She hadn't seen them in years, giving them up as babies, as she was unable to provide a safe home for them. She didn't want to die this way. The last thing she wanted for herself was to die suffering, and she had had enough of that already in her short life. In desperation, she prayed to God for life. "Please God, I don't want to die a long and painful death. I want to live. I promise I will change my ways. I will deal with my addiction. Maybe go back to school and change my ways. Please God, help me this one time. I beg of you, I don't want to die!"

As she prayed, she could feel liquid leaking from her swollen eyes. She was tired but fought the sleep that wanted to take over her. "If I sleep, I may never wake up," she thought. She had no energy, and at this point staying awake was merely impossible. "Please help me stay alive," she cried in her mind as she drifted back into unconsciousness and dreamt of Kiki. Kiki was her special doll. She had named the doll after her sister Margaret. She had given the name Kiki to her sister, and for the life of her could not recall why she had called her that. It didn't matter much, because when she said the name, "Kiki," her sister was the only one who would answer to it, and this was pretty special.

Jasmine loved her doll, and it was a lot better than her usual log wrapped in a blanket. Her doll Kiki had long blonde hair. Jasmine thought cutting it would make it grow thicker, so one day she took her grandmother's scissors and set up a style shop for dolls. She waited for weeks for the hair to grow back, but it didn't. So Jasmine decided to love her more to try make up for the hideous haircut. She remembered the clothing on the doll. She wore blue, shiny, leather-like pants, and a jacket to match; something a rich lady would wear. The irony in that was it looked like the clothing Jasmine would wear when she went to work, except Jasmine was no rich lady. Jasmine recalled times she would talk to her doll saying, "One day I will have a fancy coat just like you." Jasmine would have never predicted that, indeed, she would have a coat like this but not in the way she wanted.

Her Aunt Mildred had brought her the doll when she had come in from the big city. She remembered the night her aunt arrived. It was a few days after Christmas. Things had been terrible already with Grandfather throwing out the tree one day, and on Christmas day, throwing out the turkey. The gift of the doll took Jasmine into a world of make believe. Her world was full of happiness; there was no drinking and there was love. She played with that doll all day, then at night, she would wrap her in an old towel and tuck her in close so that no one could hurt her.

Dreaming of Kiki brought Jasmine back to the living. Her dream was confusing to her and she wondered if this was what it was like to die. Was this what it meant to have your life flash before your eyes? As Jasmine continued to think about her "dream" or her "flashback," she couldn't help but think and maybe even laugh at the fake blue leather clothing her doll had. Jasmine thought about the first time she hit the streets wearing a dark blue pleather outfit. Her pleather pants was tight. Her outfit hugged her body like a second skin. She had been nervous and wasn't even sure what she would do. She had a job to lure men into hourly rented hotel rooms, to do the deed, and then hand her hard-earned cash to her keeper, Anthony Marks.

Anthony was once her "boyfriend," but he had expectations. She first met him when she was sixteen years old. "Sweet sixteen, and never been kissed I bet," he teased as she walked by him at the arcade door entrance. She blushed and kept walking. Carol warned her about him. "He is too old and too experienced with life," Carol would say. Anthony had a car, money, and Jasmine's escape plan. Anthony's courting didn't last too long and, before she knew it, she was living at his house. Jasmine was in love. She continued to attend school, but all eyes were on her, as the one who was shacked-up at sixteen. The romance did not last long, nor did her attendance at school. Reality soon set in when Anthony intimidated her into doing what he wanted.

"Anthony should be the one here," Jasmine told herself. She hated him with everything she had. He brought her into this crazy world and now she was laying here, dying, or at least felt like she was. Jasmine wondered how long she had been here. She still had no inclination of where she was or what had happened to her. She fought to recall her actions but everything was a blur. She laid there, hoping that something would give her a clue as to where she might be. She would rest for what seemed hours, hoping to regain some energy. The day moved slowly, but as it did, her alertness was heightening and she started to hear noises in the background. Prior to that, she had thought that maybe she was deaf too. She still couldn't move her head, but at least now, she could faintly hear someone or something. "Fucking Anthony! I hate you! You need to die, not me!" She felt tired again but was determined to fight to stay alive.

She tried once again to move. Underneath her body, she could feel things poking into her. She was on an uneven surface with things poking into her exposed skin. She definitely was laying on something but could not figure out what. Every movement was painful and, at this point, she concluded that some of her bones were broken. "What the hell happened to me?" she cried in her mind. She could not answer her own questions. Instead, she laid there thinking of how she was going to get herself out of this mess. Jasmine's energy level was low, and her ability to stay awake was hard. She thought of her sister Margaret. Margaret was not her real blood sister, but because Jasmine's grandparents raised her, Margaret became her sister. Margaret, although a lot older, filled the role of being a good sister.

She knew Margaret would tell her to stay awake, and to fight for life. She remembered something Margaret said to her when she was dying of cancer. She said, "Living is hard, but knowing you're dying is harder." At this point, Jasmine's tears started to pour and there was no stopping them. She thought that if she died today, she could at least be with her sister. She decided at that moment to make peace with God, just in case. As Jasmine prayed, she faded back into unconsciousness. Was God taking her this time? She tells herself that she's prepared to go, she knew now that this time, her sister would be waiting for her, just as she used to wait for her.

Jasmine drifted back into a memory. This time it was summer. She loved summer. When her grandparents drank and fought, at least she could sleep outside in the makeshift shelter her grandmother had made in the woods. When her grandmother wasn't drinking, she too would go out there to sleep. Together they would huddle under the canvas in hopes that Grandfather would not find them. When both grandparents were drinking, Jasmine would go find the shelter. She would take her special blanket and curl up in the shelter. Some nights it would be cold, other nights it would be toasty warm, and some nights it rained. This one time, Jasmine remembered a storm hitting in the middle of the night. She was glad Grandmother was there that night.

Jasmine's sister Margaret did not live with them. She had her own family, and they lived where the tower was a few miles down the road. The tower was high, and during the summer months, men would go sit up there and watch for forest fires. The distance between the tower and Jasmine's house seemed so far away to a four-year-old. Her grandmother did not drive, so they would have to walk the distance. The walk seemed to takes days, but in reality, it was maybe an hour. Jasmine always remembered that tower. It was orange and looked like a small house attached to the top of the wooden structure. There were windows in all directions. Jasmine thought that if she climbed up the tower, she would be in heaven. The fascination of the tower always lured Jasmine's attention. Her sister would tell her that sometimes at night, when the moon was out, she would climb the tower and touch it. Jasmine would never question her sister. Instead, Jasmine would smile in wonderment and decided that one day she too would climb that tower and touch the moon.

Jasmine jolted back into consciousness with a familiar sound ringing in her ears. It was birds, and they were squawking at her. Ravens, crows, seagulls, she was not sure, but one thing she became sure of was, she was in a landfill. She was in the landfill! "Oh my God!" she cried in silence. "How the heck did I end up here?" Suddenly Jasmine's heart started to race. She was going to die! She was not sure which was going to be more painful, the suffering of just laying here in heartache and regret, or being picked apart by dumpster birds; scavengers appreciating their next meal. Still unable to move her limbs, Jasmine fought to open her eyes. The pain was almost unbearable, as if someone had sliced her eyes open and had poured in peroxide. The more she fought to open the squint of her eye, the more pain she felt. She knew she had to keep trying and soon found that her left eye was catching the gleaming sun.

The sun's rays pierced like daggers, but she fought to open it wider. Seeing the sun had not been a surprise; she had felt the warmth of it. She guessed that it was high noon, as the sun was piercing straight down onto her. Its brilliance was unbearable and found that closing her eye would be best. She asked herself, "How the hell did I end up in this shithole of a life?" Her girls. My God, her girls. What would they think? Or would they even remember the crappy mother she had been to them? Maybe this was God's way of punishing her. With all her hardships and bad luck, maybe this was the price for giving up her children. She recalled the words of her grandmother explaining the gift of children sent to us by God to cherish. She wondered if maybe this was why her biological mother had died a slow death from alcohol.

Jasmine could not die here, not today. She tried her best to wiggle her body in hopes that she could at least feel something. Anything. Everything seemed dead; her arms, her feet, her legs, her torso. Dead. Jasmine guessed that it might be Sunday, as the last day she recalled had been the Saturday before. There was no one around, nor would there be until tomorrow. Dump shopping had been once a privilege for locals who would go and take what others had thrown out. It didn't mean they were poor, it just meant they knew how to recycle and reuse things that would otherwise go to waste. When new laws came in for dumps, they fenced and gated garbage dumps. Jasmine had rationalized that this was the government's way to keep the Indians out of there. Closing the dump was extreme, and now that closure would cause her death. She was afraid that if no one found her today, she might not make it through the night. Her greatest fear was to be this helpless and vulnerable, and to be eaten alive by wild animals.

Jasmine knew in her mind that she had to try something; to scream, to move, anything to convince herself that she would live. She would live, and she would give herself a chance in life. Jasmine tried to swallow, hoping she could get some saliva moisten her throat so she could scream. Her throat was dry and she was dying from thirst. She needed water, just a drop of water, and maybe just a drop of hope. She opened her eye again to see if there were any signs of anyone, but there was no one, just the ravens scavenging close to where she was.

She decided she would focus all her energy on trying to move her body. She concentrated hard and thought of herself as a superhero with great powers. There was a numb feeling, and parts of her body felt detached. She still felt warm, and told herself this was good. She fought hard to move, to wiggle, and to squirm, but her energy was low. She stopped to takes some deep breaths, and tried again. Her body was broken, her emotions in fragmented pieces, and her soul was ripped right out of her. She was tired and decided to stop for just a second, to regain what little energy she still may have left.

Jasmine drifted back into her childhood; a place that was at times just as scary as it is now. She went back to that place where both peace and war existed and she thought of her sister. She missed her more now than she ever did. When times were hard for her, her sister was always there to save the day. She had been a superhero to her. Just like the superhero, she now needed to survive. Margaret was always the peace that Jasmine hung onto throughout her life. She went back to the day Margaret and her two girls moved away. Peace, that day, was far from the feeling she had. Instead, that day brought an overwhelming fear that she could never describe, not at that age anyway.

She remembered that day! That day her world turned upside down. Her sister and boyfriend had arrived in a vehicle, although Jasmine could not remember the type. They had brought the girls, Margaret's children, and a cousin named Judy with them. Judy was about twelve and sometimes would stay with Margaret too. Jasmine was happy to see all of them. It had been a good day, and no one was drinking that day. Jasmine had been by the smokehouse laying the logs in neat rows just in case her grandmother needed them. Her grandfather had been working on something by the creek. Her grandmother had been inside the cabin cleaning or cooking; Jasmine could not recall. She just remembered it was a good day. There had been peace.

"I come to say good-bye, I am moving away." Those words stung Jasmine's heart, stopping her dead in her tracks. Jasmines first response was, "Take me with you." When the answer came in as a solid no, Jasmine was beside herself, and unable to keep her composure. She started to scream and cry. "Take me with you, take me with you, take me with you." Hanging on to Margaret's hand, she begged her, "Please let me go."

Jasmine's tears awakened her. The crying had helped her open both eyes, and now she was able to confirm that she really was in a dumpster. For all of her life, Jasmine had felt her life was a dump. To end up in the landfill maybe should not have been surprise. She looked up toward the sun, to see its positioning. It was lower than it had been from the first time she was able to see it. Her experience told her that it might be between three and five o'clock. She knew it was a large range but it gave her an indication of how long she had been alert and possibly laying here. She heared the scavenging calls of the dumpster birds, but they were not near her, she presumed they found something more rotten than her body to feed on for now. She hated them at that moment, thinking they were probably just waiting for her to take her last breath before she too, became their next feast.

Jasmine worked hard to get her body moving. She wondered if planes flying over could spot her. Her laying there, naked, in a pile of garbage. The thought made her sick, and she didn't want to think beyond the naked. She closed off the idea of being a rape victim, although it would not have been her first experience. She thought about the night before she ended up here. It was a usual Friday night; drinking, dancing, and looking for the next rent cheque. Of course there was always that sacrifice for rent. The sacrifice, the self-hatred, the remorse, and disgust that came with the territory of "working hard for the money." She hated this life, but the welfare system would have starved her.

Jasmine spent the next hours trying to get some movement in her limbs; she realized that it was the only way. By now, her body felt more swollen. As the hours went by, and with every conscious effort, she convinced herself that more feeling was coming back. She imagined herself wiggling toes, lifting hands and moving her arms. Maybe positive thinking, praying, and determination would get her out. With each self-talk, she used her energy to try moving a part of her body, and soon enough she found that she could wiggle her toes. She continued to wiggle them until the numbness slowly left. She was more determined now to try the rest of her foot. She was still confused as to why her body felt so detached, and questioned if maybe she had been drugged.

After all, she was a street girl, and things like that do happen. She thought about that little altercation she had that Friday night with a girl named Candy. "Candy, what the hell kind of name is that?" Jasmine had laughed when Candy was introduced to her. Candy did not take to Jasmine's sense of humour and pushed her up against a wall. The ladies exchanged a few words but had left it at that, and had each moved to separate sides of the bar. Jasmine wondered if Candy had been involved in her demise. "Mind you, this could be anyone's doing, but mostly mine," Jasmine thought. Just as quick as her optimism was up for survival, her low-self-worth would swoop in and tell her that maybe she wasn't worth being alive. With her spirit crushed and her body hurting, Jasmine fell back into her sleepy state.

Like a book, her mind picked up where she had left off from the last little sleep; her sister saying good-bye and Jasmine screaming for her not to go. She remembered her sister taking her by both hands and holding them gently. They walked toward the back of the cabin She knew her sister was trying her best to calm her. When she had calmend down, she asked her sister, "Where are you going?" Her sister told her that she was going to the moon.

"But that's so far away." Jasmine told her.

"Not that far," her sister responded. "And at night when the moon is out, you can wave at me. I will look down and wave back at you."

Somehow knowing that she would have this contact with her sister, calmed Jasmine. She remembered standing on the road waving, as her sister and her family left to start a new life somewhere else without her.

Jasmine woke up again, and it had become darker. She must have slept for the rest of the day. She had no energy; every ounce she had, had been drained trying to move her body parts. She was unsuccessful at moving. Her only hope now was to wait and pray that someone would find her. She felt more alert, but still unable to move the parts of her body that would allow her to walk out of here. She laid there, listening to the night. As it got darker, Jasmine noticed the big, orange ball above her head. The moon.

Jasmine stared up and, for that moment, she felt totally disconnected from the earth. She stared into the tranquility of calm and imagines her sister standing there, waving. With the little physical energy she had, she lifted up her hand and waved back.

THE RACE

Patty was tired of it all. She was tired of hiding, tired of lying, and tired of living. Anywhere from a pill addiction, the vodka, the beatings, the cheating… Patty was just tired. There was nowhere to go, nowhere to hide, and no energy left to plan her escape. Patty had convinced herself that her family would be fine without her. She and Max lived away from everyone, and they really didn't keep in touch anymore. She had been swallowed up by his life. She had felt as though she was drowning in quicksand, and there was no way out. The end had to come soon.

These last years had been the toughest. Max was drinking more than ever, and the beatings were getting worse. The last one landed her in the hospital with a broken arm. She lied and said she had fallen down the stairs. No one ever questioned her injuries, and she knew no one truly cared. This town was not for people of her skin colour. Max had the right colour skin, and this was always his ticket to freedom, at least in this town. She had tried to convince Max to move to the north, but he would not even consider her idea. At least in the north, she knew people, her type. She had yearned to go back to that familiar place of catching fish and cooking it on the shoreline; that place where at night the northern lights danced your troubles away. But they were stuck in this one horse town with all its conveniences: a bar, a tire shop, a grocery, store, a café, and a small hospital that catered to the local farmers. It had been even too small for Patty to find a job, so she stayed home alone and waited on Max.

This morning had been no different than any other morning. Patty woke up, cooked Max his breakfast, packed him his lunch, than sat and smoked five cigarettes to go with her half a pot of coffee. Max was quiet that morning, and she knew that he was up to his usual charming self around town. She actually didn't mind his cheating. She had hoped that maybe he would really fall hard for the next girlfriend and leave Patty, but this was wishful thinking. Patty would laugh each time he would come back and "love-up" on her.

She would sometimes tease him and say, "Sad when no other woman wants you." This of course would piss off Max, but his ego would be too bruised from being dumped by a skanky barfly that he would just pretend he didn't hear her rude comments. Patty knew that if she hadn't already paid the price for her smartass remarks, the piper would collect later. And so, she drank vodka all day and popped her pills at night to numb the world from around her.

It was a beautiful morning, and summer was just settling in. The leaves had coloured the landscape green, and the grass had blended nicely. It was as if someone had come in with a large paintbrush and stroked paths of green so that the earth's colours would match. Patty sat on her porch, drinking her morning coffee, smoking her extra-long thin American cigarette her friend, Maggie, had brought her from Las Vegas. Somehow, she knew in her heart that today was the day. The long lingering look into her back yard told her that someone beyond would be waiting for her today, and so she decided to make the commitment.

There really was no other way out for her, and she really had nothing to lose anymore. She carried her own burdens, and they had grown too heavy. No other person really understood the agony of this sort of pain. And Max, well he was just an added burden; a burden she managed to kill off with her vodka and pills. Patty had no children. Her brothers and sisters were off living their own lives. Nobody would be at a total loss. A few would miss her of course, but they would soon dry their tears and move on. This was her life, and she was done living it.

After making her decision, Patty took her time and moved back into the house. She tried to convince herself that maybe today was not the day. Maybe she had her timing wrong. "No, everything is as it should be," Patty told herself. She stopped in the bathroom and perched herself on the sink counter and looked at herself in the mirror. "Well, hello nothing!" she said to herself. "Just wanting to say good-bye to myself." She got off the counter, stood in silence, and opened the medicine cabinet. In her collection, she found a variety of anti-depressants, anti-anxiety pills, painkillers, and sleeping pills. She stood there staring at the collections and laughed.

"Imagine the end-your-life TV commercial I can write with these right now. If you're sad, can't control your anger, in pain and can't sleep, you're shit-out-of-luck, because none of these pills will work unless you take them all!" She laughed hysterically for a second then very slowly began to empty the containers. She held out one hand and used it as a scoop, the second as an opener. Very slowly, she opened the pill containers filled with "no hope", "shattered dreams", and "broken promises" and placed them in her hand. "Three of these, six of these, a few more of these, and a few of these, just for good measure," she told herself. She felt the stillness of her quiet home. It was peaceful, and soon she would join its serenity. There really was nothing left for her.

Patty moved to the kitchen, to where the dishes were piled up from this morning's breakfast. "Looks like someone will actually have to clean-up after himself today, fucking loser," she sputtered as she stopped to find a clean cup. "Such a jackass. I can't believe I wasted my life this way. He made so many promises," she continued muttering. Patty found her favourite cup with the saying, *Don't worry, be happy*, written on it. She had purchased it at a thrift store during a trip to the city one day. It reminded her of her grandmother, who would say that to people who were feeling down. It was actually cute, because her grandmother knew very few English words, so saying, "Don't worry, be happy," was her way of communicating in a positive way.

Patty took the cup and proceeded to wash it, then stopped and laughed at her gesture. "What, suddenly I'm afraid of germs or bacteria," she laughed to herself, and she opened the tap and poured her water. Patty walked to her kitchen, sat on the old couch then, very slowly, swallowed a few pills at a time.

Patty decided to go back to bed. She wanted to at least look like she was at peace, when someone, well probably Max, found her. She didn't care what his response would be, didn't care if he cried, and didn't even care if he gave her a proper funeral. In her mind, she had already died so, so long ago. Patty closed her eyes and prayed that this would be easy, and painless. She prayed that it would be as simple as just drifting into dreamland. Fatigue had found her. Suicide was without stress. Patty laid down, closed her eyes and began to reminisce about her childhood. She thought about the time her grandmother left for a long time. That feeling of solitude was almost unbearable but somehow she had managed to survive. Why couldn't she be that strong kid she used to be? "I guess that strong little shit died too, a long time ago," she thought.

Patty drifted back to her old hometown, Molanosa. She remembered the time she had stayed over at her Auntie Joan and Uncle Arthur's house. They had been kind enough to take her in during the absence of her grandmother. She didn't like the idea of staying alone with her grandfather, and so she begged Joan to take her home with her. Joan had a kind heart. Taking Patty home would be best, as Patty would not have far to walk to school, and she would have other children to play with during this difficult time. Joan and Arthur's house was grand, at least it seemed through the eyes of a six-year-old, and in comparison to her small one-room, plywood structure cabin. It had many different rooms for different activities. There was a room just for eating, and another for sitting and visiting. There was a bathroom inside their house, which was a luxury to Patty. There were two or three bedrooms. In Patty's mind, this was how rich people lived.

Patty had never been away from her grandmother before, and there was an overwhelming fear that she was not coming home. From her six-year-old perspective, this would be the worst thing ever that could possibly happen.

To Patty, Joan and Arthur were good parents; the type she would have liked to have. Instead, her mother had handed her over to her grandparents. They drank quite a bit, but she loved her grandmother more than anything and would not have traded her now for anyone else. Still, each time she went to Arthur and Joan's she did not see them drinking. Arthur didn't seem like the type of father who would ruin a child's Christmas by throwing the tree or turkey out. She sometimes wished they were a family like this. Arthur loved his children, and Patty had seen that through the laughter they shared together.

Patty had slept alone on a single wooden bed off in the corner of the house. A woodpile laid just off to the side not too far from her and close to the woodstove. Patty was not used to sleeping alone and Joan and Arthur's three children had already occupied the bedrooms, so there really was no room for her with them. She remembered Arthur quickly making her the bed using plywood boards and two-by-fours that had been laying in his yard. She remembered waking up feeling lost, lonely, and empty inside. Her first thought was to cry but the other children had already been up and were calling for her. She had to be strong. She told herself that her grandmother would be home in no time, and she would go back to snuggling with her. It had only been two days, and Patty was already feeling the loneliness settling in.

Patty wondered why she went back to that memory; surely there had been happier times. Oh yeah, like the time she and her grandmother were forced to sleep outside in a make shift shelter, she reminded herself. That life was so long ago, and her grandmother always tried to protect her the best way she could. She was a child, and she had left that place and time so many years ago to marry a man who would change her life forever. The task of closing her eyes and calmly slipping away was just not happening the way she had planned. Her childhood memories seemed to want to stay with her for a while.

Patty wondered, "Why am I rehashing these memories? Am I supposed to reverse what I just done? Are they telling me that I was tough then, be tough now? Why are they loitering around in my mind like that drunk guy at the local gas station that annoys everyone?" Holding up her hands to touch her eyes, she wondered why life dealt her this hand. Her eyes were dry, and they had been dry for some time. Her pain had numbed her ability to cry, and her lack of care gave her no reason. Since the moment she had decided to end her life, her mind seemed to be in a tailspin for what seemed liked days, but soon enough it would come to a halting stop. Patty continued to close her eyes in hopes that the effects of the pills would soon take their course. As she laid there, her memory of childhood continued to play on.

Patty went back to the time she stayed with her Aunt Joan. She remembered one particular morning so clearly like she was watching a television show. She had just finished breakfast and was eagerly waiting to get to school. It was sports day and this meant racing her friends and hopefully winning some ribbons. She remembered Joan calling her to the sitting area, and handing her a bag. She opened the brown paper bag and inside found the most magnificent gift a child could find for a day like this. The bag contained a brand new shirt, matching shorts, and the best part, a pair of brand new running shoes. "I hope you fit the shoes, your grandma gave me the size when we drove her to the hospital the other day." Everything was perfect, and even if she didn't win any ribbons that day, the brand new clothes were the best prizes.

Patty wondered if this was the way Christmas felt. She wondered if this was the way other children felt when they were opening their beautifully wrapped gifts from under the tree. She wondered if they felt so happy that they might explode. She never ever forgot that feeling from that day. Thinking about it actually brought tears to her eyes. She realized how much her grandfather had taken from them, from her and her grandmother. She realized how much he would have taken from his three biological children, who ran away from home from the time they were able to.

Patty woke up from this memory and was finally starting to feel a bit more tired. She looked at the clock and saw that it was already two in the afternoon. Max would be home at six. Maybe. She really didn't care anyway. She was feeling the effects of the pills and her head was starting to hurt. She was tired, and so she laid there, hoping that soon all this would end peacefully. She closed her eyes and saw images of herself running. "Aw, the race," she whispered, "that was quite the race!"

"Keep running! Run faster! Go, go, go!" She could hear the cheers from the crowd standing along the race line. Patty was running as fast as her legs will carry her. She looked to her right and spotted Annette and next to her, Bernadette. Fast runners they were, but Patty was just a bit faster today. All three girls, head to head, racing to the finish line. Up ahead, Patty saw the bright orange ribbon stretched across the finish line. In just a few seconds, she was going to break through that ribbon, and she was going to be the first one to do it. She could feel the victory, and her heart was pumping hard. Her feet were like feathers and she felt as though she was floating in the air from her speed. Patty kept focused on the ribbon; there was no looking back.

She saw two people holding the ribbon, one on each end. Their faces were forgotten as the blur of time had taken their identity. On the other side of them stood a man. As Patty raced closer, she recognized that it was her grandfather. Before Patty could even cross the finish line, tears started to stream down her face. Her grandmother was not there to watch her and, suddenly, she realized how lost she felt. She pushed forward. She longed to see her mother's face but she was gone. She pushed herself as others gained to try to catch up to her, but this win did not mean anything to her anymore, because her grandmother was not there to see it.

Patty awakened, and nausea had set in. Was it from thinking too much of her grandmother that was making her sick, or were the pills digesting? She felt shame, and knew that her grandmother would have never approved of her taking her own life. Patty looked at the clock again, it was three o'clock. She was still coherent, but was feeling as if life was slowly draining from her. The memories of her grandmother were playing on her conscience, and she started to cry, "I am so sorry Grandma, but there is no other way." Patty touched her face, and felt the wetness. The wetness from tears that came from a place where hurt, pain, and truth were found. But also tears that came from reminders of resilience, hope, dreams, and love. She closed her eyes again, and floated back to that day. She went back to that day when her first real memory of violation surfaced.

Patty remembered winning the race, but somehow the momentum was gone. She remembered her grandfather standing there on the other side of finish line holding out his hand. It had a quarter in it. A shiny silver quarter. She was afraid to go to him, afraid he'd take her back home, to where they would be alone.

Patty laid in her bed, weakened, but not weak enough not to remember. "This truth! This truth will die with me," she quietly sobbed. She tried to live out her life in a normal way. But how could she? She didn't even know what normal was, nor what it was supposed to feel like. Normal. Normal was for those who had a mom and a dad and little brother that came from the same set of parents. Normal was going to church with family then enjoying a nice meal after. Normal was the ability to sleep and not have the dreams to haunt you. Normal was living in your own skin and loving that no one had violated your innocence. As she laid there thinking about that race, she knew in the end, it was the race that had beaten her. This memory had her by the throat. The truth. The pain was unbearable. She was afraid, but not of dying. She was more afraid of remembering what happened to her as a child. She was just a child. An innocent little girl, who just wanted to be loved, and to have a family without alcohol or abuse. With all that had happened, she was sure her grandmother would forgive her for this.

Patty stayed laying in her bed. She had no energy left. She wondered if it was true what they said about those who took their own lives. Was she going to hell? Her grandmother had become a good Christian woman, so she guessed that she would have been in heaven. Patty prayed to God for forgiveness in hopes that he would let her through the pearly gates so she could be with her grandmother and with others she had lost along the way. She knew these were the last few hours of her life and felt confused.

As she laid in her sweat-drenched bed, she felt more tears coming. She cried emptiness for a long time. The tears actually felt good. She almost felt alive again. She felt sick and felt her stomach twisting. She took her blanket and held it close to her face to absorb the tears, the other half, she tucked into her stomach to help with the pain. With the little energy she had left, she looked up at the clock and it read six o'clock. She quietly closed her eyes and whispered into the quietness, "No regrets, Patty. No regrets."

HEARTACHE WRAPPED IN A BOW

Wendy had lost track of time. The snow on the ground and the worn calendar hanging in the dining hall were her only indications that Christmas was just around the corner. She had no schedule. She wasn't going anywhere anytime soon. In fact she would be here for about another seventeen hundred days. She still had over four years left on her manslaughter sentence. Time was just time. She had been no stranger to the justice system, so a long prison stay was not surprising on the day the judge laid down the law on her. Wendy was actually surprised she had only received eight years, but wasn't going to argue.

The way she had seen it, it was eight years of not worrying about where her next meal would come from; eight years of knowing where she would sleep, and eight years of not having to listen to the bullshit whining of society. "Sure glad I don't have to listen to the… 'the poor need to be fed, the youth need to be jailed, the Indians need to be educated, and the government… Oh my God we need a change and the rich need to be richer', and so on and so on," Wendy would convince herself.

Wendy had grown up in a string of foster homes after being apprehended by the state when she was only eleven years old. Her one and only attempt to leave a bad situation had led her to another, and the trail hadn't stopped since. She spent a total of five years in care and had actually enjoyed her last home until her foster mother passed away in a car accident. Wendy was to be moved shortly after the funeral, but decided to check herself out of the system permanently. She lived from town to town, city to city, and from fight to fight. She was tough, and not too many messed with her. This was what survival looked like for Wendy. She had a lot of friends, wasn't in any gang, but somehow could not get that break. The "break!" The "break" everyone talked about and wished for. The "break" everyone complained about because they just could not catch it. Wendy spent her earlier years bouncing from one waitressing job to the next. When she realized working the bars was more profitable, she quickly switched careers. The "profits" came with a price. Slinging booze meant throwing out drunks, breaking up fights, and sometimes having people swear at you. Then, of course, there was dealing with the perverts that hoped to catch a "break".

"As if!" Wendy would shout at them, "Go home to your wife and kids." The highlight of her job was the long hours she worked. Long hours meant more pay, and more of a cut on the tip money.

Wendy tried hard to be a good person. The type of person her grandmother wanted her to be, but it was hard. She had a temper, and losing her temper under an alcohol-induced state was common. Wendy figured her assholeness must have come from her grandfather. He had filled her anger bucket to maximum capacity, and then some. Wendy had long concluded that it would take more than a lifetime to empty it, and maybe a couple of lifetimes to get an apology for everything her grandfather had done.

Her grandmother had left with the parting words on how her grandfather would live a long time because he needed that time to see the pain he had caused on his family. And pain he did cause. He caused enough pain to cry a river. Wendy had kicked out Crying a long time ago, and had allowed Anger to move in. Anger decided to recruit Tough, so Tough moved in and hadn't left since. Together Tough and Anger gave Wendy the confidence to survive. She would tell herself, "I am so tough, even Chuck Norris is scared of my tears." Then she would laugh and think about another ten corny Chuck

Norris jokes. If anyone ever asked who her superhero was, it was Chuck Norris all the way. But deep down inside, this was not who Wendy was; it was who she had become to live and survive. There were days that her grandmother's teaching of love and her values would shine through, but Wendy was careful. The last thing she wanted was for someone to take advantage of her well-hidden good nature.

Lately, thinking had been a great pastime for Wendy. She would spend a good part of her day in her cell reading, writing, or thinking. The other time was spent visiting with her new best friend, Shelly. Shelly was in for six years after she ran over a child while impaired. Wendy didn't ask her about this; she was sure Shelly was suffering in her heart and in her mind. Sometimes in the middle of night, she would hear Shelly crying. Wendy knew it wasn't from the loneliness, but from her remorse. Shelly was a small, little woman, weighing in at about a hundred and twenty pounds. Sometimes the other girls would try to rough her up, but with Wendy on her side they would back off. Wendy wasn't afraid of anyone. Her two hundred and fifty pound frame could match almost anyone in that joint. Shelly and Wendy got along good, and this helped the time pass. They had been cellmates for just a little over a year and had now started to bond more like sisters.

Wendy and Shelly woke up that morning and poked fun at each other for the type of day they were going to have. It was "craft day". They had both speculated that Christmas crafts would be the theme, so they both decided on making snow people. Wendy would make the man and Shelly the woman. They spent a few minutes laughing on how the snow people had better behave, or getting hot and bothered would melt them both. They both got ready and headed down to the dining hall for breakfast and, as usual, they were the first in line. They had the schedule of getting in line before the other inmates perfected. Being late meant not getting enough to eat. As they were approaching the dining area, a guard came up to Shelly and said she needed to be escorted to the station. The station was off limits, and often only visited for bad news, or news of early release. Wendy knew that early release was not an option for Shelly. Shelly left with the guard as Wendy watched, wondering what was going on.

Wendy finished breakfast alone then proceeded to go back to her cell. When she arrived, she found Shelly in a fetal position on her bed, sobbing.

Her face was covered, and Wendy knew in her heart that something was terribly wrong. She knelt close to Shelly and gently wrapped her arm around her. "It's okay, you can talk to me." Shelly, hardly able to spit out the words between sobs, managed to say, "My mom ... there was an accident ... Mom's gone."

Wendy didn't push further. This was devastating to Shelly. Her mother, Rose, had come to visit a few times, and each time Shelly would cry for a few days after. Rose was a good person, but Alcohol and Drug Addiction had become her best friends, and she couldn't seem to lose them. In fact, Drug Addiction had overpowered Alcohol, and had become the main tenant in Rose's body. Shelly laid there sobbing, and Wendy felt something she hadn't felt for a long time; helpless. She knew there was no way to take away this pain her friend was suffering. Wendy decided to leave Shelly for the rest of the morning in hopes that Shelly would regain her composure and come find her later. She told Shelly that she'd save her a seat in the activities room for when she came down later. Shelly laid there sobbing without responding to her. Wendy was not even sure she heard her.

Wendy slowly made her way down and wondered if leaving Shelly was the right thing to do. She didn't know how to help her and knew she maybe couldn't. It was hard to see someone hurting and crying the way Shelly was. It brought back memories of the night Wendy had hit Kurt hard enough to kill him. He had been in the bar roughing up his wife again, and Wendy had warned him. Mostly Kurt would laugh and say, "And you're going to do what?" Most nights Kurt was escorted out. But that night, the bouncers were nowhere in sight, so Wendy took matters into her own hands.

She remembered warning Kurt to lay off his wife, but like the jerk he was, he turned to hit Wendy. Wendy had been no stranger in the ring. She clenched her fist and, as hard as her weight would throw her arm, she nailed him right between the eyes. She nailed him so hard, he fell and hit his head against the metal leg on the bar table. Blood came pouring out. Kurt's wife was standing there, screaming as loud as her lungs would allow. Wendy stood in silence. Frozen.

What happened next was a blur. All Wendy could recall were the sobs of the woman who had just lost her husband. He was the man who beat her, but he was the man she had loved. Somehow, Wendy didn't fuss too much about the eight-year sentence. She took a life and had to pay. It bothered her more to know that a child's life was worth six years to a drunk driver, and an abuser's life was worth eight.

Wendy ended up in the activities area alone that afternoon. She saved a seat for her friend, but her friend never did make it down. Wendy spent the afternoon making her a dream catcher with some nice feathers that she had dug up from the bottom of one of the craft boxes. One feather was pink. That one would be Shelly's mother, in remembrance. Wendy spent her afternoon sitting alone and worrying about her friend. She prayed with the dream catcher in hopes that the prayers would follow into Shelly's dreams. She knew Shelly was up for some tough days. Wendy wasn't sure how she would help her, so the dream catcher was the best she could come up with.

Later that afternoon, Wendy went back to check on Shelly. Shelly was sitting up, but did not look like she really wanted to see or talk to anyone. Her eyes were puffy and her face was red. Wendy went and sat beside her on her bed. With her arm draped over her friend's shoulders, she handed her the dream catcher. She explained how she prayed into it and had placed the pink feather in remembrance of the mother she had just lost. Shelly took the dream catcher in her hand and held it. She leaned into Wendy's chest and, while clenching the dream catcher, she sobbed some more.

All Wendy was left to do was hold her friend until she was ready to stop. Shelly cried for a bit but regained her composure to thank Wendy for such a special gift. "No one has ever done anything special like this for me. Thank you." They sat in silence for a while and then Wendy suggested they go down and sit in their favourite spots for supper. It was a bit too early, but Shelly was up for getting out of the cell and walking for just a bit. They left their safety nests, as Shelly clutched the dream catcher in her hand.

They walked down to the common area; a place where other inmates hung out and watched television, played cards, or just sat and talked about things they were going to do when they got out. It was usually busy in there at this time; most would have just come in from their privileged outdoor walks. Rain or shine, snow or blizzard, no one passed the opportunity to be outside, even if it was for just a few minutes. Wendy and Shelly walked in and went to where a group of fellow inmates were playing cards; poker to be exact. It was the better choice of groups to go and spectate, as the poker players enjoyed displaying their skill of deceit to one another. There was only one rule for the spectators: be quiet when watching. No talking. They stood there quietly and watched the serious, straight faces of "I can out-bullshit you with these cards." The atmosphere was intense and the stakes were high. The ladies liked to play for cigarettes, snacks, or with whatever they owned that someone wanted. The only rule the players had was you either left the table with nothing or everything. It was winner takes all. Wendy and Shelly walked on to the spectators' ring to watch the last six out of ten players battle it out. They watched quietly as the first three cards were laid down. There was some betting but most folded, leaving three to play. Tensions were felt and, as a spectator watching, Wendy could see the solemnness of the stares. Outwitting, bluffing, it was their game… Fourth card, the turn, had a few really fired up but they all kept their cool. Wendy chuckled to herself, "The perfect game for a group of scammers and con artists." The fourth card was an ace that forced a player out, and left two at the table. They sat there staring at one another. No emotion, full eye contact.

"All in."

"I call," was the response back. Before anyone could say anything, one of the girls grabbed Shelly's dream catcher, and ripped it out of her hand. "My good luck charm," she shrieked. The pink feather that Wendy had meticulously place on the dream catcher, fell loose and floated very gently in the air. Wendy watched in disgust as the feather looped around and made its way down, hitting the floor. The impact crushed Shelly's heart and triggered Wendy's anger.

Without thinking, Wendy reached over and flipped the poker table, sending all the chips scattered on the floor around everyone's feet. The room became so quiet that all that was heard was the last chip spinning and then landing on its face. Wendy, now looking down on the woman, took her pointing finger and placed it smack on her forehead. No words were said; the message was clear. Before Wendy could finish her message, the guards were there to grab her.

Wendy found herself in 'the hole'; a place she hadn't been to for some time. She hated the confinement of the place. It reminded her too much of times spent sleeping under beds to hide. The hole often brought back childhood memories that had haunted her. She hated remembering those times because it usually meant two things: either her grandmother was being beaten, or

Wendy was left to her own means and found safety sleeping under beds. The hole' was not a nice place, and Wendy had tried her best to avoid being there. The only good thing about 'the hole' was that she was quite sure there would be no mice visiting.

The last time Wendy had ended up in solitary confinement was after a food fight in the dining room. The fight had started because of bad cooking and not because of bad behaviour. She remembered hating the place so much, she had vowed she would not be back. And yet, here she was. Wendy knew that this time it would be a longer stay, so sleeping her time away was definitely her only hope of surviving her punishment. She loved to sleep, and she knew she could never catch up to the many all-nighters she had pulled many moons ago. And so, sleep came easy. Doing twelve hours meant half of her day would be done.

Wendy looked around the cell she would call home for the next few days and wondered how people stayed sane in here. Four, white walls. That was it. Four, white walls. This was not going to be easy and she hoped that they would at least come tell her what her sentence would be. She hated surprises and hated waiting on others. The guards were positioned on the outer walls of the cells, so talking to them was not even an option. There were no other cells nearby, no neighbours, and no noise. Wendy hated quiet. It scared her. She remembered waking up as a child a few times under a bed, and it would be quiet. Dead silence. She recalled making her way upstairs in her house to sometimes find the front door open and the house empty. The party would move in the wee hours of the morning, leaving her alone. Wendy hated thinking about those times. They were not always good, and they drove her to the crazy life she had ended up living.

Wendy hated not knowing how long she would be in here, and her makeshift of a hearing would not be for a few days. She wondered if charges would be laid and wondered if her time would be extended. She wondered how Shelly was doing. All this thinking was not helping her. She felt weak and nauseated. Nauseated to a point that even her supper did not look appetizing. Wendy did not know what time it was, and wondered if going to bed now would mess up her inner clock. She felt tired and decided that taking a nap may help with the fatigue she was feeling.

Wendy laid her head on her pillow. She closed her eyes, but the darkness and the silence were too much. They absorbed her, and she hated the confinement. She craved the openness, and the freedom to wander even if it was in her own small cell. At least in her cell there was noise. Wendy closed her eyes again, but with the promise that she would chase away any thoughts that tried to creep into her mind and haunt her. Her mind took her to places, to times, and to events. The mantra of memories played like an old record player, stuck. "Why?" Wendy wondered, "Why?"

She had been a prisoner of her memories, and now a prisoner of society. She often questioned why she was always being punished. "Am I really that bad of a person?" She would ask herself. She often thought that maybe in her past life she may have been someone evil, and this round was about redemption. Wendy laid, looking up at the white ceiling, and tried to imagine images dancing. Just like the northern lights would when she was young. She associated the lights to peace, and somehow knew they guided the spirit to a place where the soul could rest. It was these peaceful souls that would come dance, and tell us they were home. Wendy wondered if her soul would find the lights when her time was up.

Wendy was tired and emotionally drained. She was uncomfortable and starting to feel pain in her chest. Her arms felt as though they were falling asleep, and so she laid there shaking and rubbing them. She hollered from her bed at the guard, but she was not sure he could hear her. Fear was creeping up on her, and she was not sure if this was normal. Maybe she was having an anxiety attack. She remembered having them as a teen. She would be frozen, unable to move and someone would have to call an ambulance.

Wendy thought going to sleep would help, but each time she closed her eyes, it felt as though her whole chest was caving in. Wendy tried to get out of her bed to get help, but she was short of breath and did not have the energy to stand. She hollered again, not sure if she was heard. She laid back down and tilted to her right side, hoping to breathe better. Everything seemed out of focus now, and Wendy very slowly walked into her childhood like a dream.

Wendy could not comprehend what was happening, but realized she was standing in her old living room and looking at a Christmas tree. It was as if she had floated back in time and was reliving a part of her past. Wendy remembered this moment. It was a Christmas memory she had wanted to delete from her mind permanently but found it impossible.

The Christmas season had started as always, with her and her grandmother decorating a Christmas tree. Wendy, however, had lost all hopes of ever having a "normal Christmas." Wendy would play those Christmas's in her mind and would pretend that her family had no alcohol, opened gifts, and would have big turkey dinners with everyone laughing. Instead, Christmas always ended with something bad. Mostly, there were no gifts under the tree as the money would be spent on wine and whiskey. Sometimes, there would be turkey, but it would be shared with whomever had passed out there the night before. One time, they didn't even have a turkey as her grandfather had thrown it out the door. Wendy hated Christmas, but standing there in that room, reminded her of the time she almost had the best Christmas ever.

Her grandmother had gone to La Ronge to shop and left her at home. Her grandmother arrived that night with packages and had quickly rushed them to her room so Wendy would not see. Wendy remembered feeling a knot in her stomach when she had realized that for sure she was going to have gifts under the tree. She remembered her grandmother wrapping the gifts and the next day laying them under the tree. Wendy recalled sneaking under the tree, gently taking a gift and shaking it, while her grandmother was outside. One of them was a Monopoly game. She was sure of this; the box size confirmed her guess. Wendy was beside herself. She wanted that Monopoly game so bad.

The day before Christmas, Wendy woke up optimistic. "Maybe this year Christmas will be different," Wendy thought. She had always wanted what other kids in her community had: Christmas with a tree, a turkey dinner, and presents. She went about her day, walking on clouds, knowing she had gifts under the tree. She remembered going to visit friends for the afternoon then coming back to a house full of drunks. Wendy had been devastated but would hang on to the hope of the morning when she would open her gifts, namely her Monopoly game. Wendy continued to walk through her memory. This time she was at her cousin's house. She recalled the events that led her here. Her grandparents had packed up her gifts in a green garbage bag and had taken them to a cousin's place. She was told she would open her gifts with the other children and that they were spending the night there. Her grandparents had been drunk by this time, and Wendy would spend the evening crying. To make her feel better, her cousins would take her to their rooms to play cards. Wendy remembered falling asleep and waking up to laughter. She remembered springing out of bed to rush to her gifts. When she got to the living room, her heart fell. The other children were sitting on the floor playing Monopoly. Her game. The only gift she had wanted. Her grandparents were nowhere in sight. She asked about the gifts. She was told that they had been traded for wine.

Wendy stood there, looking at herself. Her childhood. Her trauma. As she looked into her own face, everything faded and her chest pain was gone.

Wendy could hear voices, "She's having a heart attack, clear the room!"

STELLA COYOTE

Many knew Stella, and everyone who knew her had loved her. She had personality, spunk, and a charm that just grabbed your attention. When Stella was around, everyone wanted to be in her presence. Her laughter could fill a room. She was funny, adventurous and never stayed long enough for anyone to get bored with her. She was constantly moving from one city to the next, hoping to find the prince charming that would sweep her off her feet and settle her down. Stella had found a few frogs, but kissing them did not awaken the Prince. So, she stayed single and mobile.

She made her home across the provinces, visiting and living from one friend or relative to the next. She was a free and wild spirit. She lived life writing her own rules. No one really knew how she did it, but she always managed to find some sort of odd job that would keep her going. She never really had a whole lot of money, just enough to appease her love of cigarettes, vodka, and a bus ticket to the next destination and adventure. Stella always paid her way. She was not one to take advantage of others, and she didn't depend on anyone but herself. Stella was tough. She was the kind of woman you wanted on your side.

Stella came from a small town. She grew up with instability and constant movement. Attending school became problematic, as she would finish one grade at one school then another grade at another school. This continued until Stella was in high school when, finally, the alcohol quit flowing in her house. By this time, she had learned to be tough and had already established her own set of rules. Stella found it hard to follow rules made by others, so she made her own. Rules had always been grey when Stella was growing up, especially at home. When she found herself in trouble, she had learned and mastered the art of lying. At the age of ten, Stella had already been introduced to alcohol. At the age of fourteen, she had become good friends with Mary Jane. She liked her marijuana. She soon learned to live the life of deceit by hiding her drug use.

To everyone, Stella was a free spirit who lived life on her own terms. Some would tell her that she had the best type of life: no commitments, no strings, and the freedom to do what she wanted, when she wanted. Some days this was true. Most days, Stella just wanted to stay in one place. She wanted nothing better than to just have her own family, her own space, and her own sense of peace. However, this lifestyle had swallowed her up and she was caught in a funnel. Stella would not show her wounds, so she continued to live her life on the edge with everyone looking in with admiration. Maybe it was deceitful, but it was past the point of no return. She did not know how else to live. At some point, Stella had accepted that she did not choose this life. This life had chosen her. Stella moved within it hoping that the change of scenery would give her new hope, but it never did. Her routine became habit and her habit her life.

It was an early fall morning when Stella woke up from her cousin Rhonda's house. She looked out the window, and through its thin glass, she could hear the geese flying above. She had been visiting there since summer. The sound was her warning signal to move back west to warmer climates. Stella had been working as a housekeeper with her cousin Rhonda at the hotel and had managed to scrape five hundred dollars together. This would be enough for her bus ticket to Vancouver and maybe enough for food and supplies for a few days. She knew Tina was anticipating her arrival, and she looked forward to returning to Vancouver. Stella had grown accustomed to life without snow, so trading it in for rain was okay.

It was mid-October when Stella boarded the bus. It was always a long bus ride to Vancouver from the little Saskatchewan city. Stella was not looking forward to it. The bus rides always gave her time to think. Most times, the thinking just turned to guilt. The guilt was not for what she had done but was more towards things she did not do. Today's bus ride would be no different. She sat in the front of the bus; away from the younger people who liked to crowd to the back. The driver was satisfied with just driving the bus, so Stella did not engage in small talk with him.

It was early when the bus rolled out. Stella was still tired from the farewells from the night before. She had the full seat to herself, but soon realized that all the other seats were full. Stella hoped that her luck with the seat would not change and that they would lose more passengers than gain. The first few stops were a blessing. No one got off, but no one got on as well. Stella enjoyed the freedom of stretching out her legs and sleeping between stops. It would be a twenty-four hour trek and the trip included a few transfers along the way. Stella knew sleeping would be the best way to pass the time. She also knew that the comfort of not sharing a seat was not a guarantee.

Her first transfer landed Stella the good fortune of enjoying a seat to herself. Her last and final transfer, however, was not in her favour. Stella found herself having to move to the back of the bus, and sat with a stranger who she had hoped did not want to talk. Stella regretted sneaking to the local pub between transfers, as she was now stuck sharing a seat. The ride this time seemed to last forever, but as luck would have it, her seat-sharer got off at the next stop. Alone again in a seat, Stella fell asleep and did not wake until dark.

Stella had slept hard this time. She did not even notice the next woman that got on the bus had made herself comfortable next to her. Stella woke up to a face looking down at her. The woman's eyes sported familiarity. "Sorry, I hope I did not wake you," the woman said.

"No, not at all," Stella replied as she stared cautiously at her. There was something so familiar about the woman. Stella could not put her finger on it.

"I'm Nancy," the woman said, extending her hand to Stella. Stella accepted the handshake and extended her hand back. As she touched the woman's hand, Stella felt an unusual peace flood throughout her body. She knew this woman, but she could not recall where she may have met her.

"I know you from somewhere," Stella announced.

"Of course you do," Nancy replied.

"So where do I know you from?" Stella continued to ask.

"We've never really met, but we know everything about one another," the reply came. By this time, Stella was worried that either the vodka had finally kicked in from a few stops ago, or she had just met the creepiest person ever.

Nancy continued to talk to her asking, "Do you remember the time you thought your grandfather axed your grandmother to death?" How could Stella ever forget? It had been raining that night. Her grandmother had been babysitting the neighbour's son. Her grandfather hadn't been home for a few days. They knew he was drinking around town. She had prayed he would stay away until he sobered up, giving her and her grandmother some peace. She hated the alcohol that had lived with them. The nicest times were when her grandmother was not drinking and would go on "the wagon." However, those wagon rides never lasted; it always seemed that, at some point, the ride would get too rough and her grandmother would always fall off. It was during one of these times when her grandmother was not drinking that all hell broke loose.

That night lived with Stella. Each time she thought of that night, it always seemed like yesterday. The images were still clear in her mind. Her grandmother was in the living room, sitting on the floor, and playing with the little boy she had been babysitting. Stella recalled how she went to the washroom after her grandmother had asked her to wash her hair. She had removed her shirt so that she would not wet it while washing her hair. She had just placed the shampoo on her hair when she heard her grandfather coming in through the back door. She could hear him yelling at her grandmother, and her grandmother asking him to be quiet so that he would not scare the child playing. The next part of the memory always took her back to the point where she ran out of the bathroom to see what was going on. Stella thought that maybe the noise had startled her to run out of the bathroom. What she witnessed next was an image that would forever burn in her memory.

Just like a photo one does not want to see, Stella clearly remembered the image of her grandfather, standing above her grandmother, with an axe in his hand. Her grandmother was now sitting on the floor holding the little boy on her lap, looking up. The fear on her face always brought tears. Stella remembered standing there screaming, and then running out the front door without a shirt on and her hair full of shampoo. She still recalled how she ran across the road in the pouring rain to a nearby teacher's house screaming, "He killed her, he killed her!"

The second part of the memory had always been a blur to Stella, but she always remembered how relieved she was when her grandmother walked through the door while holding the little boy. Stella recalled how the RCMP later showed up and escorted her grandfather out of the house. Stella snapped herself out of the memory only to find herself sitting alone again. Stella sat and wondered about her life. She wondered about Nancy and wondered how she knew. Stella decided to get off the bus at the next stop and made the decision to find herself. Stella decided that finding Lost would be her next adventure.

THE ROAD HOME

It was a beautiful summer day when my husband Glenn and I decided to take the drive to Molanosa. in memory, Molanosa was my first home. This was where the hurt started, so this was where the healing had to begin. Visiting the place where our old family cabin stood was a trip I had planned for some time but lacked the courage to take. I would often find reasons to delay the journey each time my husband would suggest it. On the day we made the decision to go, I felt strong and knew that I now had the strength to face whatever memories or emotions were waiting for me. I knew I would have the strength to face them, because I knew I would not have to face them alone. I had love and support on my side and I knew I could do this.

The road to Molanosa is less travelled, but somehow we managed to pick up a hitchhiker. I knew the man. He was still living in Molanosa long after all other residents had moved across the lake to the new community of Weyakwin. His family's cabin was just a few hundred metres from where our cabin stood by the creek. Sometimes he would go to La Ronge to visit; when he was done, he would make his way home to Molanosa. I was unsure of where our old cabin stood, so it was nice that he needed a ride as he was able to direct me to the exact spot where I had once lived.

As we approached the area where I once lived, my husband walked in with me, hanging back a bit to give me the space I needed. The area had grown in somewhat, but there was evidence that the area was still being used. The creek that was close to our cabin looked different, but the muskeg to the west held familiarity. A canoe lay on its side close to the creek. I assumed it belonged to the man we had given a ride to. I went and stood by the creek and looked into its waters. As I stood there, I closed my eyes and imagined myself as a young child getting into a canoe with my grandmother, then tipping the canoe over. My grandmother shared that story for years, telling everyone that I had loved the reflection of my face in the water, had looked too hard, and managed to tip us over. She would laugh each time when she told of how she had to fish me out of the creek, soaked, wet and crying. As I stood there thinking of that time, I cried again knowing that not all memories were bad. I now had the task of taking the good ones and using them to heal.

I don't know how long I walked around the old site remembering my life in Molanosa. I found remnants of a life lived rusted, buried, or broken. I found an old blue glass jar that I immediately recognized as the Noxzema my grandmother would spread evenly on her face. She would then walk around the old cabin with its aroma following her and filling the air with an unforgettable fragrance. Next to the Noxzema jar was an old broken wine bottle. The image of my grandmother breaking a bottle over my grandfather's head surfaced and I felt tears welling in my eyes. In the relics laid an old, metal dipper rusted from the years of exposure to the elements of nature. It had been used to scoop water from the barrel that sat close to the door covered with a clean, white sheet.

My grandmother was always careful about placing the white sheet to ensure no ashes or other debris would enter into the drinking water. As I continued to walk, I came upon a rusted out roasting pan, half in the ground and the other half exposed. It was at this point I broke down and remembered the horrific Christmas of my grandfather beating my dear grandmother and later throwing the turkey out the door. The roaster laid stuck in the ground just as it did forty odd years ago in the snow. There was no turkey laying next to the roaster, but somehow my mind allowed this image in and it was clear. I felt a cold breeze hitting against me, just as it did when I was a child running out without a jacket in the middle of winter.

As I sat there and cried, my husband approached me with a plastic crate he had found and handed it to me. He told me that maybe I should pack up the items and take them home with me. At that point I was not sure what I was going to do with them but thought maybe the answers would come. The ride home trekked into more memories; many were set off by being at the old home site. As we were travelling along the grid road, I shared a story with my husband that I hadn't dredged up in years.

It was fall, and grandfather had been commercial fishing. It must have been a payday because I remember him holding a stack of money and telling my grandmother he would take us all to La Ronge to shop. I always had mixed emotions when we would go because two things were a guarantee: junk food and alcohol. Nonetheless, it was an outing and there was nothing wrong with praying that this time they would not drink. Of course, my prayers were never answered. I figured God didn't really listen to four-year-olds anyway. It was raining when we left, and the trip took longer than usual on the old grid road.

We arrived in La Ronge and headed to our shopping spot: Vanco's IGA. It was a big store, for a four-year-old, and I remember the clothing area very clearly as it was always my first stop. Being as poor as we were, having a brand new piece of clothing meant the world to me. It was a ritual: me with clothes, grandma with the groceries, and grandfather sitting next door in the bar "waiting for us". The event that followed was always pretty much scripted as well. My grandmother and I would pack up the vehicle, and she would then go in the bar to "get grandfather". I would wait in the vehicle just for her to come tell me that he was not done yet and that she would "stay with him" until he was done. Most times, I would sit in the vehicle waiting alone into the night. Grandma would come "check up" on me now and again and usually with a bag of chips and a pop. This was how it was. On this particular trip, I remember heading home with my grandfather driving while he is drunk. I remember falling asleep and waking up to a sudden jerk of a hand moving across from me. My grandmother and grandfather were yelling at one another. We were in the middle of nowhere; it was raining and they were fighting. I remember screaming at them to stop, but their screaming towered over mine and I went unheard. I remember my grandfather stopping the truck, coming to the passenger side, and opening the door. My grandmother was trying to fight him off; I was screaming as he dragged her out into the rain. I remember looking through the back window at the images moving, one image on the ground and the other standing. I remember crying but was too scared to get out of the vehicle. I remember my grandfather jumping back in and driving away as fast as he could, leaving my grandmother on the muddy road in the rain. I was scared, thinking he may have killed her, so I started to scream as loud as my lungs would carry the sound. He stopped the truck and drove backwards, but grandma was not near. He jumped back in, drove in reverse and stopped again. A few minutes later, grandma crawled back into the truck, soaked and bloody. I could never erase that image, as young as I was, but had stored it away until that day.

We continued our journey home with less emotional and hurtful stories. But as we drove down the grid road, I realized how entrenched my life was on this beautiful land I called home. My stories laid where they were created. Buildings may move, landscapes may change, but stories stayed forever connected. As we got closer to La Ronge, I wondered if maybe this was why I was uncomfortable in La Ronge. A lot has changed, but yet when I was near certain sections of town, memories tugged at me, and some were not so great. The worst ones were those near the bar where I spent many nights crying as my grandparents sat inside and drank.

Other areas of La Ronge held fond memories. Although there were huge houses sitting in the areas my cousins and I used to play, the great feeling of being with family never really left my soul. When I drove by the areas, I imagined myself as a little girl running through the forest playing a good game of hide and seek. My older cousins knew all the trails and, within minutes, we would be from one relative's home to another. Yes, there was drinking, but I was cared for by older cousins and they seemed to help the sadness disappear, if not just for those moments.

Deciding what to do with the remnants of my past was without a solution for the time being. I figured that believing the answers would come when they needed to, they would. A few weeks after the trip, I met an Elder at the grocery store and we got to talking about my return visit to my past. He told me that I must begin my healing process through ceremony. He gave me specific instructions on how to enter this elaborate, yet meaningful, practice. He instructed that I go only when I was ready; when that time came, I would know. The boxes sat in our garage for two full years before I felt ready to start.

The waiting was not a timing issue, but rather a time to grieve, a time to cry, and a time to conceptualize what forgiveness may feel like.

The two years it took to enter in ceremony were the hardest two years of my life. Not that the years prior were easier, but I had become good at blocking and ignoring memories. It was also during these years that I was diagnosed with Bipolar II disorder. There was a lot happening in my life. I had a lot of support. Many tears were shed and there were many long nights of loneliness. Did I contemplate suicide? Yes. Many times... but the thought of missing out on watching my grandson grow into a young man halted any attempt I may have conjured up. During this time, I felt a rage brewing inside me, but I kept telling myself that I had survived the worst of it already. I needed to gain strength to face truths I had buried so well.

This was when I really found praying. Using sage to smudge was soothing and peaceful. I knew I did not have the power or the strength alone to face some of those demons. I strongly believe that I was guided from something stronger than man... a higher being... the Great Spirit. These two years were spent convincing myself that I had purpose, I was worthy, and that life was to be lived and not destroyed.

CEREMONY WITH ANNA

It was once again a beautiful fall day when my husband and I decided to drive to Molanosa. I had waited for this trip for a long time, not really knowing when the time was going to be right. On that particular day, it felt right. There was preparation for this trip in more ways than filling the gas tank. I had to ensure my spirit was strong and that I had the emotional strength to do this. I knew I was ready. I took the time to smudge the items and prayed as I held each in my hand. They held memories of my past and they carried with them stories that hurt my spiritual, emotional, mental, and physical being. As I smudged each item, I carefully placed the item back in the milk crate I used to bring it home. We packed a lunch, my camera, some cloth, and a shovel. I also took my sage and some tobacco. I had anticipated this trip for some time and I felt nervous to reach my destination. After all, it is not often one buries the hurts from the past in a more literal manner.

The drive was beautiful, as Mother Nature had painted the land with orange, red, and yellow. The air was damp, as the sun was hiding behind the clouds. There was a hint of gloom, and it was as if what I was feeling in my heart had manifested itself into the weather. As we got closer to Molanosa, I spotted a young eagle on a tree. I asked my husband to stop and back up so that I could get a picture of it. He backed up slowly as I prepared and armed myself with my 300mm lens. The eagle stayed perched on the tree long enough for me to take my shot before it swooped up and flew straight down the middle of the road. I quickly jumped in my truck, opened the sunroof, and told my husband to drive. I continued to take pictures of this magnificent bird from the opening of the sunroof. The eagle continued the routine of flying ahead of us, landing on a tree to wait for our vehicle to catch up, then swooping in front of us, flying ahead. The eagle did this for about five kilometres. I asked my husband to stop and I made a tobacco offering to the eagle. After the offering, I got back into the truck and we drove. This time the eagle continued to fly on, heading west into the tree line until I lost sight of it. I knew the eagle was there to guide me. This was my sign that my journey to heal had started.

We drove down the dirt road that led to where my home once stood and parked up on a hillside. Looking down, you could see the creek that flowed through Molanosa. My first home was right around the corner. I walked on from this point alone. I walked, carrying my memories in one hand and carrying the shovel that would put some to rest in the other. I also shouldered my camera bag, along with my cloth, tobacco, and sage. The walk was a quick few minutes and I soon found myself in the clearing where our small house once stood. This place was familiar, as I had been here a few years back, picking up and sorting through memories that either made me smile or made me cry. I walked to the creek and found a plastic tub laying on its side. I sat and looked onto the water for a bit, not really knowing how to proceed with my ceremony. I stood in silence looking around to where our canoes once laid on their sides. I couldn't help but think about my thumbnail that was deformed from trying to climb one of the trees that were surrounding me. I looked around and wondered which of the trees were missing the piece that lodged into my thumbnail, killing its root, and leaving me to fashion my extra thick nail. My mind played with me for a moment and bounced from one childhood memory to the next; some sad, others that made me laugh. I decided to proceed with the ceremony I had come to perform. Standing here and reminiscing could take up not only the day, but my emotions as well. I slowly paced back to where I had laid the items from my past that I would soon bury. The shovel laid patiently, as if telling me that soon it would participate in something powerful. I picked up the shovel and held the wooden handle firmly and knew that I had come here to release my burden. After burying the items, I sat and cried. I was not sure if the tears that fell were coming from a child who suffered trauma or from the adult who was wrestling with forgiveness.

After I had completed the ceremony to heal, I sat and thought about Anna. I had started writing this story long before the ceremony. The writing of this story became dependant on me actually moving forward in this healing journey (if that makes any sense). In a million years, I don't think I could have written about characters if they did not exist in one form or another. To me, they exist. Although I do not live as they do, I could have easily walked that path. For some reason, life did not allow me to take the journey that Anna was given. Call it luck, fate, or chance. I call it purpose.

As I thought more about Anna, I thought about my biological mother. I remembered the last time she had moved to Prince Albert, Saskatchewan. She went on the bus one day and promised she would come home. She did, only so that I could place her in her final resting place at the age of fifty-one. She had succumbed to her disease of alcohol. I remembered a time where I had begged her to please find a house and get us children back. I wanted that family so bad. I wanted to live as the family that sat and played Monopoly for hours, then fought because one had bought out all the dark blue properties.

When my grandma (mom) and I would go to Prince Albert, I would look at the houses we would pass in our taxi rides and pretend that she was taking me back to Rose (my biological mother). I would imagine a big surprise party waiting for me with all my brothers and sister. They would run to the door and tell me that my arrival had now completed the family. This never did happen and somehow I had accepted that it was not supposed to. I realized that this turn of time, and my history, may have been the one that could have ended me as Anna. Later in life, as I watched Rose drink herself to her grave, I was grateful that life did not give me what I wanted and, instead, put me where I needed to be. I accepted the fact that the Creator had a different plan. Maybe the plan was for me to give to those in need. Maybe the plan was for me to have good listening ears so that others could talk and not be judged. Maybe the plan was for me to drive around cities handing out food to the many Anna's who needed a meal. Maybe the plan was for me to write and share my story, and to encourage others to break free from their hurts. I am not really sure what the ultimate plan is, but I live each day feeling thankful and blessed.

I realized over the years that Anna lives within me. In fact, I believe Anna lives in many others as well. Sometimes I drive to the river here in Prince Albert and I see the Annas of the world. She is not just a person that lives in the figment of my imagination. She is real to others and she is hurting from a history that has destroyed so many in its path. When I look and see people on the streets struggling, I can still see my mother Rose. She lived that way for years. I think about the many nights she might have slept outside, too drunk to find her way home. I think of the men that might have violated her and sometimes even beat her and left her in some back alley. Sometimes mom (Jean) would get a call from the hospital telling us she had landed in there. We would always catch the bus and go see her. That life could have been mine. All it takes is one decision, one move in a different direction, to set anyone on Anna's course.

As I sat for those moments in the peace that the land was giving me, I felt as if a certain shadow was near. I was not afraid. I knew that this shadow was a part of the burden I had carried. I also realized that I had buried the items within a close proximity to where my grandfather (dad) had thrown out the turkey. I placed my hand on the ground and prayed that things like this would not happen to other children. Though the memories are real, Anna is a symbol of where I could have ended up. Those memories belonged to my grandfather, my beloved late grandmother, and myself.

The memory of Christmas when my grandfather beating up my grandmother and throwing out the turkey had happened. I wish that somehow I could erase it from my mind, but I can't. So, instead, I want to share the story to unload the burden. That day in Molanosa, I brought my burden home. My ceremonial journey placed the burden back to its origin. That day, I put it back for the land to heal.

To this day, I don't really like the taste of turkey. I will not eat it unless it is smothered in cranberry sauce. I never really thought much of this connection. Growing up without really having to eat certain foods just didn't grow on me. In fact, I cannot even remember my first real turkey meal. Sad, isn't it? The things many people take for granted are some things others never had or experienced. There are many other food habits I have. I will share this story.

My two girls and I were eating a bologna sandwich one day, when my husband walked in. We had just finished placing the bologna in the bread and squishing it tightly between our hands, making a fist motion. He asked why we ate our bologna sandwiches this way, and the girls told him it was the way I had taught them. I hadn't really thought about it until he asked at that moment. I sat for a moment, and like someone had just put a re-run on television, I flashed back to my childhood and imagined myself walking into the store. Very slowly I shared my story with my family. It was a story I couldn't share without a tear falling. It had been so long since I had thought about it. I told them that when I was younger, I was hungry a lot. I had become good at stealing to survive, and one tactic I mastered was stealing bread. Bread was filling to me and it could get me by for a few hours. I knew already as a child, that stealing candy would get me caught as it was always in the front of the store. The bread was always in the back. I would go to the back, quickly open the bag, and take out a few slices. I would place the bread in my hand, squish it in my fist, and put it in my pocket. It was also a good idea to place the plastic bread clip back on. Once outside, I would take the squished bread out and eat it. I guess the added bologna was a symbol that I had made it. I had money to buy something extra to add to the squished bread. Something I had wondered about was the people who later bought the loaf of bread I stole pieces from. I wondered if they realized they were only getting nineteen slices of bread instead of twenty-one. And if you are wondering, no, I never ever took the bread crusts.

THE MOON, OUR CONNECTION

It has taken me months to get myself to write this chapter, to think about Jasmine and the Jasmines of the world. More importantly, to think about the Indigenous women who, for some reason, walked out of their family's lives, never to return. They have become the pile of tears many families have shed for their loved ones. I dedicate this chapter to all these women who are mothers, sisters, aunties, cousins, or friends. I could not even imagine the turmoil these families feel, not knowing where their loved ones are. I also dedicate this chapter to my beloved sister. Margaret Brown, who was born my aunt, but because her parents (my grandparents) were the ones who raised me, she was my sister and I only knew her as that.

Margaret was my friend. The relationship she and I had went beyond what everyone really knew, and beyond what many might not understand. Margaret really was my saviour in many ways. She was the keeper of our family secret. When she had passed away, I will admit that I was angry that she had left me holding the ball. She left this earth, and I was left holding this big ugly secret alone. At least, prior to my healing journey, this was what it felt like. In all fairness, and in hindsight, I don't think this was something we should have had to keep a secret.

My memories of Margaret start in Molanosa. There is no recollection of her ever living with us. I have memories of her visiting, then later living in a small house with her husband, Gilbert. Margaret always paid special attention to me, treating me more like I was her daughter than her niece. I loved having her around. Margaret lived with Gilbert at the conservation officer's house. It was a small hike to go visit her. I remember knowing we were near her house because I would see the house in the sky. It was orange and it had always been my dream to climb up into it by climbing the ladder that led into its doorway. I would often stand, staring up, and thinking that it went right up into the sky. My sister, noticing me, would tell me that at night time, she would climb up and touch the moon. I believed her. I wanted to touch the moon too.

I remember the day Margaret came over and announced that she would be leaving with Gilbert. She would no longer be living near us. I remember crying, wanting so badly to go live with them. Margaret had two baby girls, and I know now that she needed to look after them first. I cried and threw myself on the ground, hoping my temper tantrum would get me my wish. I remember clearly that I was crying and asking where she was going. She held me, pointed to the sky, and said she was going to the moon. She told me to look at the moon when night came, to wave at it, and she would wave back. For days to come, I had stayed up waiting for that ball of orange to appear. I would wave and convince myself that she really was looking down at me. Over the years, I knew she really didn't go to the moon. Yet, the moon became a place where I looked upon when my life became unbearable, as Margaret was no longer there to make the monster go away.

When I was a young girl, I would sleep between my mom and dad (grandparents). Sometimes, if they hadn't been fighting, we would go to bed and they would be drunk. I would wake up to the moaning and grunting of them having sex. I had blocked this from my mind for years, as each time, the thought of this would make me sick to my stomach. What's worse are these very vague memories of me being touched by him. I am not sure what to make of these memories. Are they real? I know what I am about to write is the truth.

When I was about eight years old, I had made a bed on the floor of the living room in our house in Weyakwin. There had been people sleeping in all the bedrooms after a party. When I mean party, I mean the kind where there is beer, whiskey, and whatever else people would drink to get drunk. I remember there were two couches and Margaret had passed out on one of them. I remember feeling pretty safe because she was nearby. In the wee early morning hour, I felt a hand in my pants and I awoke, startled. I jumped up and yelled for Margaret and found my grandfather hiding under the blankets. Margaret jumped up, suspecting what he was doing, and started kicking him in the ribs.

I don't recall too much after that, but I remember Margaret telling my mom that she would take me to live with her in Buffalo Narrows. I remember feeling shame for so long. Then one day, not feeling anything; numb from disgust. I would cry and Margaret would wipe my tears away, telling me that she would never let him do that to me again. She never told anyone. It was our burden. It is now my burden alone. I don't think anyone that hasn't suffered abuse can ever really understand this. The shame sits in the pit of stomachs; self-hatred hides in souls, and tears flow when no one is looking. I am not just talking about myself; I know many feel this way. This is why many choose not to talk about sexual abuse, or incest. It hurts to talk, but it hurts more not to. I guess this takes me to the understanding, and empathy, of why so many choose alcohol or drugs to numb the pain. I am not saying it solves the problem, I am just saying I understand why.

When Jasmine came to me, I had been thinking about the crap our young Indigenous women endure. I was thinking about how marginalized Indigenous women are. In traditional Indigenous societies, women were the ultimate keepers. They made the final decisions, and they were respected to the highest regard. They were keepers of song, of ceremony, and of medicine. I think this is why we (Indigenous women) continue to survive. Our grandmothers continue to send us strength. I believe this is why I continue to survive. When I smudge, I sense and feel the presence of grandmothers. I feel their strength. When I smudge, I send smudge prayers to all women. I pray for the women who have not yet realized the source of their strength.

I think about my past self-destruction. I hated myself so much that consequences of my actions were not a part of my thinking pattern. I drank. I did drugs. I got into vehicles that maybe I should not have gotten in. I think about the time I ran away from home. Imagine that: grade six, running away to a big city. My aunt Nancy did not know I was arriving on the bus that day. What if the circumstances gave me a pimp taxi driver and took me to a place where they sold young women for prostitution? It could have happened. What if I met some nice lady on the bus and she offered to take me to her house? I probably would have gone with her. What if she ran a prostitution ring? At any point in time, I could have ended up in a situation like Jasmine. I could have been looking up at the moon, praying to see my family, my sister.

My sister has gone to the spirit world. I often wish that she could have stayed a bit longer so she and I could sort through this together. She had so much pain in her life that she numbed herself with alcohol. This is such a common story; I hurt, I medicate. I talk to her when the moon is full. For the nights when the moon is not full, I had left a glass moon on her grave and keep the exact same one on my lawn. The moon, it is our connection. At night when it is full, I wave, and she waves back.

THE MAKING OF STELLA

I don't really remember exactly when Stella Coyote came to me, but I am not one for boring presentations. I was working for my band, the Lac La Ronge Indian Band, when I was asked to organize an in-service for teachers. I wanted to wake everyone up with a good laugh. I decided to dress up as a crazed woman named Stella. I am pretty sure I might have thought of her character long before, but never had the opportunity to bring her to life. I had put on some high boots, a wig, and cheap makeup. I walked into an auditorium full of teachers, waiting (I am sure) for yet another monotonous episode of "in servicing". I don't think anyone was prepared for Stella. What I was less prepared for was how her character would become me within seconds of putting on her clothing. She was tough and feisty, but still had a great sense of humour. She organized the workshops with her canny remarks, her jokes, and her stories. Everyone loved Stella. In fact, she was loved enough to be invited to other gigs for pay. Stella never took up any offers. She lived on her own terms and decided on her own appearances; paid gigs did not appeal to her.

When I got home from work that night, I made a Facebook post about my friend Stella Coyote. Coyote of course, came from the animal that was neither fox, nor wolf. The fox is beautiful, small, and sharp. When I see a fox alongside of the road, I can't help but to look, wondering what colour it will be. Sometimes, if I am lucky, I will spot a fox that is a bit black in colour. I think it is a silver fox. If and when I do come across a wolf, I am mesmerized. This animal is the king of the four-legged creators, in my opinion anyway. A wolf is strong, intimidating, and a leader. A coyote is… well, it's a coyote. I don't look their way in awe but rather out of pity. I know I shouldn't feel sorry for them. They are survivors, much like Stella. They are scruffy and not the most beautiful creatures, but they have those dark markings around the eyes that make them seem lonely. Kind of like Stella. Also, I really think the name Stella Coyote has a nice ring to it as well.

Stella became a Facebook personality for some time. I would post about how she would call me from odd places and would share stories of her misadventures. My Facebook friends would find entertainment in this. If I didn't post anything on Stella for some time, a few of my friends would ask how she was doing. I often wonder what figment of my imagination she came from. I wondered, if life had sent me a curveball, if I would have been tough like Stella. To me tough and strong are really two different things. I think "tough" masquerades hurt, and "strong" is fighting through it. I am still not sure which is better. To be have been "tough" may have spared me some heartache, but to be strong leads me to a better life. I just wish that sometimes it were not so hard.

In 2015, I was diagnosed with bipolar disorder. I always suspected that I had some issues, but bipolar disorder was not one that I would have put on my list. When I first received my diagnosis, I was in utter disbelief, but after some time of thinking about some of my behaviours and moods, I really should not have been surprised. I struggled and continue to struggle with highs and lows, and sometimes my Stella persona kicks in. Her toughness is what really helps me get through some days. Prior to my diagnosis, I am positive Stella was with me. I think back to some of the temper flares I had, and I am almost certain I used "Stella" for my protection. Don't get me wrong, I am not stating I have split personalities, but rather explaining the behaviours I exhibited because I was not sure what was going on with me. I have more clarity and understanding now. In fact, the first fifty pages of this book were written in ten days during a manic episode. Since then, I have been working hard to balance my life, finding healthier alternatives to healing. I choose not to use western medicines to control my disorder. I feel good that I trust in my cultural ways to heal. I think that my childhood traumas have placed me in this mental illness that I struggle with.

When I think of "Stella", I think not only about my disorder. I think about those who struggle with alcoholism, with drug addiction, and those who are stuck in situations that have robbed them from hope. I think about those who have undiagnosed mental illnesses. I think about those who carry such hurts from their childhood. It is easy to fall into darkness when there is no one there watching to see if you are falling. I have many standing on guard to grab my hand when I need. Others have no one. When I think of "Stella", I think about the children who are living in chaos and in pain. It is not fair. No child should have to suffer the way I did, and the way many others did as well. No child should ever have to grow up in silent pain.

SCHOOL WAS NOT COOL

School should be the place where children can feel safe but, unfortunately, school was the place that broke many Indigenous children. If anyone wonders why many hate the place, look at the history. Residential schools were built to kill the "Indian" in children; boarding schools were the tool to assimilate and provincial schools followed suit. Yes, that's right, provincial schools. My late sister had horror stories about some of the teachers that came to Molanosa. She would tell me of their cruelties. This practice did not change in the 70s and 80s when I attended. Imagine a child, growing up in chaos and trauma, being sent to school for the teachers to finish them off. Makes me sick just thinking of some of the things that happened to my fellow classmates and to myself.

Without naming anyone, I remember this one boy who was abused a lot by a teacher. I still think about him. One time, the teacher was lashing out on this poor boy, dragging him across the floor by the collar of his shirt, and then hitting his head against the metal desk. There was silence in the classroom as I sat there frozen, too afraid to move. I remember another time, the same boy was getting struck over and over again with long, chalkboard cleaners. The teacher kept hitting him around his head and his upper body. There was chalk dust in the air and huge brush marks on his head and body. The look on the boy's face was unforgettable, as he came up from his crouched position after a brush beating. He should have never been hit that way, and we should have never had to witness such cruelty.

The strap was popular during my years of education, and I was always a recipient of a good strapping. I talked too much in school and this was always getting me into trouble. I was also a class clown so my antics added to the punishment. The strap was a way to visit the furnace room. After school, if your name was on the "list", you would be one of the students that lined up outside the furnace room door. I still remember all the furnaces that stood on each side of the room. I walked the short distance, held out my hand in routine, and waited for the strap that came down on my hand. I remember one time looking into the teacher's eyes and telling him, "That didn't hurt!" I was a tough little kid, and they would never have the novelty of knowing they were hurting me, including the man who chose to punish us with the strap. The second blow to the hand was just as painful, but I would never let on to the pain I felt. I looked up at him again and said, "That still didn't hurt!" After my strapping, I would go outside, grabbing my stinging hands and holding them tight until the stinging left. Tears would fall from the corner of my eyes with all attempts to hold them back. I was tougher than they were, and I knew one day I would show them I was. I hated school and I hated the teacher. I hated that my life was bad at home, and it was just as bad at school.

The school years were hard. I was a scrawny, tiny kid, and I was an easy target for the school bully. I remember this one time, the teacher had left the classroom and the bully attacked me in front of the whole class. She thought it would be funny to lift me by my throat and push me against the wall, feet dangling about a foot off the floor. I would pray that bad things would happen to her. As I got older, I was challenged with the act of forgiveness, and I forgave her torments.

I spent extra time at school, after hours, as my grandmother was the janitor and I helped her clean up. If she was on one of her drinking binges, I would be the only one cleaning the school. Sometimes, I would ask my two best friends to help me. I would close all the blinds so that no one knew it was kids cleaning the school. I didn't want my grandmother to lose her job. We needed the money. When her school cheque would come in, I would guilt her into paying bills first. I always made sure our bills were paid before allowing her to have any cash that I knew was going to booze. Imagine that… a child worrying about the bills.

My educational journey took me to multiple communities. I started kindergarten in Molanosa. I remember being so scared to go in. I only spoke Cree and, at five years of age, I was still using a baby bottle. I didn't drink milk in the bottle, as I would whip up a "choo choo" with Red Rose tea. That first day of school was memorable. My grandmother dropped me off and told me to walk in. I was very close to the door when I recognized a truck pulling up. It was Rodrick Nelson. I ran to his truck and told him I did not want to be at school, and begged him to take me home. He told me that he was headed to La Ronge, so I then begged him to take me with him. Rodrick and his wife, Ruth, had a soft spot for me. I went into the truck and sat between them and off we went to La Ronge. I had skipped my first day of school.

The following year, the people of Molanosa were instructed to leave. A new community had been built specifically for them. Some families were reluctant to leave, but in the end, most of us made the move. I was six or seven years old when my sister, Margaret, came for me. I went to go live with her in Buffalo Narrows where I attended grade one. The making of Weyakwin was also the making of many horrible memories for me. My grandfather worked, and working meant he made money. The money was often used for trips to La Ronge where he and my grandmother would sit in the beer parlour. I am still not sure why my sister came, but I sure was glad when she showed up. Prior to that, the only connection I had to her, since long after she had left, was looking up at the moon at night and praying that she was looking down. I let myself believe that she must have seen what was happening, and came to my rescue.

I moved to Weyakwin after completing grade one in Buffalo Narrows. I was excited to see my new home as I heard it was a big house. I had attended school in Weyakwin for grade two, and then it was back to Buffalo Narrows for grade three. This pattern continued, with fourth grade being spent in Weyakwin. I am pretty sure that it was in grade four when the teacher had flipped out on me and wrapped my mouth and head in thick, masking tape. I was my usual talkative self when all hell broke loose. He lost it. I mean really lost it. I recall him coming toward my desk, red-faced, yelling at me for not being able to stay quiet for a period of time. He grabbed me, placed me in a headlock and excessively wrapped the tape around my head. The tape was tight, and I struggled to breathe. It was just before the lunch hour when I was forced to go home with the tape wrapped around my mouth and head. My grandmother spent the lunch hour cutting the tape away from my hair.

My sister and her family relocated to Dore Lake when I was in grade five. It was also during my fifth grade I started experimenting with alcohol. My life was a living nightmare. Between the drinking and all the horror I witnessed at home and school, I drank, hoping the nightmare would end. It was a blessing when my sister came to visit. It was during this visit when the sexual assault happened and she thought it would be best I go with her. I will never forget that move.

My grandmother came with us, deciding that maybe it was time to quit drinking. She left her job, so I knew she must have been serious. I think the guilt of knowing what her husband did to his grandchild killed her inside, because after that, she did everything in her power to make up for what he did. We detoured to Prince Albert before going to Dore Lake. I made my grandmother buy me a record player, and my first ever album, *Bat Out of Hell* by Meatloaf. I loved the songs on the album, and played them over and over again until I memorized the words. I had a great year that time. It was the best year, and the best of memories. Dore Lake was my magical place. That June, we moved back to Weyakwin. My grandmother did not stay sober too long, and the chaos started again. I was getting older now, and started thinking about life. I made up my mind that I would never live this way.

That fall I started grade six in Weyakwin. I woke up early one morning only to find a bunch of drunks passed out in the living room. I decided that I had had enough, and dug in all their pockets. I stole eighty-three dollars, found my Aunt Nancy's address in Saskatoon, and made the decision to run away. I bought a one-way bus ticket to Saskatoon on the STC bus. Thinking back now, I realize how lucky I was that this incident did not lead to something worse. Here I was, eleven years old, on a bus by myself to Saskatoon. What was scarier was the fact that I even took a taxi to my aunt's house, by myself. I replay this scenario in my head sometimes and thank my Creator for watching out for me. Imagine if the taxi driver was in a prostitution ring. I would have been an ideal target. My grandparents did not know where I was, and my aunt was not expecting me. I made it to my aunt's house, and the next item on my agenda was to chop off my beautiful, long hair; hair that I loved, and hair that was braided to perfection on days my grandmother was sober. It was also hair that she was proud I had, and so chopping it off was my way of hurting her. I convinced my aunt to let me live there, and I think I had a pretty good case as it took my grandmother about three or four days before she realized I had been missing from Weyakwin. I remember the collect call that came in that evening. My Aunt Nancy handed me the phone and said, "Someone wants to talk to you." I didn't want to talk, afraid I would be sent home. I started to cry, and pleaded to my grandmother to let me stay. I handed the phone back to my aunt, and I overheard that I was allowed stay. I also overheard my aunt telling my grandmother to maybe quit drinking. I enrolled in school at Mayfair and found it to be a pretty good experience. I went home that June. I never moved to another school again. As a twelve-year-old, I realized that having no rules could be to my advantage.

My early teen years kept me in Weyakwin and I attended grades seven, eight, and nine there. My grandparent's drinking was on and off but, by this time, I was numb to the life. Like I said before, I rather enjoyed the freedom of making my own rules. School was school. If I wanted to attend, I went. If I didn't want to be there, a group of us would go hang out around the river. In the winter, we would make a fire, make tea, sit around, and drink it. There was a certain innocence and peace while sitting out there. It seemed as if our community was miles away. I would sometimes close my eyes and pretend that everything hurtful about it did not exist.

When I was in grade 10, my grandmother finally quit drinking for good. I was happy for her, but it left me with the challenge of living my life under her rules. She had me pegged pretty well and was relentless about ensuring that I finished school. I was not a pleasant youth but, somehow, miraculously managed to finish grade 12 at Churchill High School. The years attending Churchill were okay; not great but not really bad either. At least none of the teachers degraded me. I graduated in 1986 with the minimum twenty-one credits and about a 60% average. When I received the "Most Improved Student of the Year" award, my heart swelled. It was not the most prestigious award like the silver or gold pin, but it was recognition just the same. That piece of paper told me that I had the ability to accomplish anything. I hung on to the symbolism of that award over the course of my life. I completed three degrees: Bachelor of Education, Bachelor of Arts, and Master of Education. As I write this, I am in the process of applying for a Doctorate of Philosophy degree. I am not sure where this journey will take me but, wherever it is, I am doing it for all those who think they are not able or not worthy. I am doing it for those who struggle with trauma and for those who feel lost. If ever there are any words that I could leave on this earth for you, I would tell you that, "yes, you are worth everything you can ever dream to become."

SURVIVAL

I am not sure what the laws of resiliency are but they sure applied to me. I think I survived so much of the trauma because I chose to dream of something better. I looked for the silver linings of life events; living for the great times I had as I was growing up. I was fortunate enough to have had a wonderful friend named Annette. She was one of my guardian angels, and I was blessed with a few of those. Annette would take me home when I needed a place, and her family treated me good. Yes, we sometimes got into trouble, but her mother, Clara, showed us unconditional love. Annette and I shared many great memories, great adventures, and great stories. Neither Annette, nor Margaret could be there all the time to look out for or look after me, so resilience became my friend. Sadly, resiliency is not always on the side of many victims of circumstance. Annette and Margaret were just two of my guardians; I had many more in our community. If ever the saying, "it takes a community to raise a child," rung true, it certainly was the case for me.

Survival and being on survival mode was so natural to me. I became resourceful; knowing how to steal food and knowing how to find safe places to sleep. A few hideouts I found were under beds, under our stairwell, and in the makeshift shed my grandfather had built for his snow machine. The makeshift shed was under the stairs outside and it had a door, so it was out of the elements of weather. Sometimes when the partiers became too rowdy, I would take my blanket and pillow to go hide in there. I would make a bed on the Skidoo seat and pray no one would find me. Often times I slept there just so I wouldn't be too tired or late for school the next day. The winter months were the hardest, but I was not afraid to knock on doors if things got really bad. Sometimes I would show up on people's doorsteps in the middle of the night and explain why I was unable to sleep. On a cold winter's night, and with a child on your doorstep, who would have turned them away? I later would wonder why no one called Social Services. At times I had prayed someone would come get me and place me in foster care. I suppose some prayers were better off unanswered.

Like I said, I was resourceful. At an early age, I knew the value of money. My grandmother did not make a lot of money in her janitorial job, so I had to figure out alternative ways to make it. When my grandfather was not drinking, he would host all night poker games in our house. I learned very quickly that poker players like to drink tea and eat, so I offered the service. My grandmother would allow me to go charge food on our store bill with the promise to pay it back when I turned a profit. Some nights, I made fifty bucks; for a young person, this was a lot of money. I often used the money to buy clothing, and I always had more than enough on our class trips.

Another way I made money was by selling the stuff my grandmother bought for me. Once in a while, I would buy things when we went to La Ronge to shop. I would keep the items for a while but, if I needed money, I would sell to friends or trade for whatever it was I wanted. I always wondered what a good teacher could have done with these skills. Maybe I would have owned a thriving business.

If I was not making money the legitimate way, I was doing it through other means; by stealing for the purpose of reselling. My grandmother and I used to go visit in Saskatoon when she was "on the wagon." We would go to the Army and Navy store where I would tuck in an extra shirt with the one I was to "trying on." I would wear the extra shirt under the one I was wearing and go back to hand in the one I tried on to the sales lady. I took whatever shirts I stole back to Weyakwin and sold them for a small fee. I am not proud of that chapter in my life. As an adult, I promised I would pay back society through generosity and voluntarism. I would like to think that I have paid my debts, and everything I do now is because it is the person I have become.

I started driving at a very early age. I am not sure how old I was when Margaret and her family moved to a farm in Paddockwood, but that was where I learned how to drive. Margaret and Gilbert had five girls and one of them, Valerie, was younger than me by a year. Gilbert used to take us out to the field to teach us how to drive. He was a great driving instructor. Valerie and I would not only learn how to drive with the chicken coop car; we were taught how to drive the tractor as well.

I have to explain the chicken coop car. Margaret and Gilbert were raising chickens and, for some reason, they decided to rip out the chairs in an old car, hook up a heat lamp, and use it for incubation. There were feathers and poop all over the car but it ran and it always had the keys in it. This one time, we were out on the field picking rocks when Valerie and I decided to start up the chicken coop car and took it for a little ride. It was very hard driving with the bad smell lingering and without any seats, so the ride was very short. Gilbert later taught me how to drive a truck with the gear shifter on the steering column. They called these kinds of trucks "three on the tree." After that, all other vehicles I learned how to drive were standard. It was a good skill for me to have learned because when my grandfather was drinking, and my grandmother wasn't, I would drive us to Paddockwood using grandfather's old car or truck. I didn't have a learner's licence, but I knew how to sit on a pillow and how to wear a ball cap to hide my face. I drove for two years like this. At the age of sixteen, I received my driver's licence.

Survival guided me to believing different things. I was scared of growing up. Growing up meant I had to take care of myself. So, I thought that the next step in life was to find a husband. The fear of not having the ability to look after myself pushed me to marrying my first husband at the age of eighteen. Neither of us were mature enough for the adult game of marriage, so the marriage did not have a "happily ever after" ending. It ended, but not without being gifted with the two most beautiful beings I had ever laid my eyes on, my daughters Jamie and Criss.

My other means of survival was my use of drugs and alcohol, but mainly, I stuck with the drugs. Having a driver's licence had some setbacks; I would be the designated driver at times. I wasn't going to risk my licence, so I would smoke pot knowing the high would wear off faster than the alcohol. I also had the idea in my head that the cops couldn't test levels of marijuana for intoxication, so I led myself to believe that I had the system beat. Also, in all honesty, I had never heard of anyone being in a vehicle accident while under the influence of MJ. When I was fifteen my grandmother quit drinking. I found my marijuana use was easier to hide than if I had been drinking.

Fifteen seemed to be that magical age where everything happened. My grandmother quit drinking, and I was in high school. I had other issues, I am sure were related to being an adolescent, but I hit a time in my life where I just did not want to live anymore. In and around the time Grandmother quitting drinking, I felt lost. I was scared of growing up, and yet I wanted to be an adult. I wanted to have control of my life, but I didn't know how. No one ever told me I could grow up to be independent. No one told me I could build a life for myself through education, and so with no hope of a future, I decide to end it all. I still remember that day I stole all the Tylenol and took the whole bottle. I can't remember how many pills there were, but I remember it being a large bottle. What I did not count on was my grandmother's addiction to pills. She had replaced alcoholism with pills. Or maybe this was her escape for having to live with the brutalities of my grandfather. Whatever the reason, I didn't count on her missing her pills just a few short hours after I took them. She found me downstairs in my room. I laid in bed, waiting for the pills to work. She angrily stormed into my room, yelling, "Where are my pills?"

"I took them all," I responded in fear.

What happened next tore my heart in two and, for years, I lived with the image of her screaming at me for taking her only pills. She was not concerned that I had taken the whole bottle of pills as a means to die. She was only concerned that she did not have anymore pills left. In her anger, she told me to get up and go upstairs with her. She prepared me a warm glass of water with salt and told me to drink fast. I drank the water, not because I wanted to save myself, but because her rage scared me. I drank the salt water and soon found myself throwing up all the pills. The vomiting was so intense, the blood vessels broke in both my eyes, and I looked like shit. We never spoke of the suicide attempt again. It was then that I thought I was in this alone forever. But, something changed in my grandmother. Maybe it was the scare of my dying, but we never talked about it. Somehow my attempt brought us closer together, and it felt like it was love. From that moment on, she began to share things with me. She would sit and share stories of long ago. She would tell me about some of the things my grandfather had done to her. Sometimes her stories would trigger my memories, and I don't know if that was a good thing. The good thing though was we had each other for love and support.

GRANDFATHER

The day I was called to come to the Long-Term Care facility to sit beside my "father" (my grandfather) was a day of mixed emotions. I knew eventually I was going to get the call that he soon would leave this world, but I guess I pretended he had left already. I sat by his bed looking at him, helpless and weak. I had convinced myself on the drive from Prince Albert that I needed to forgive him. He needed to hear the words before he left this earth. I wanted to assure him a safe and healthy journey back to the spirit world.

I arrived early that afternoon and sat next to him. I took his hand and held it in mine. He opened his eyes and, noticing I was the one sitting there, a tear fell from his eye. I knew the end was nearing and I had to say the words, "I forgive you," even though I wasn't sure if I had even convinced myself of it. I held his hand and, through my cracked voice, I said it. I told him I loved him and had forgiven him for everything. I assured him that mom (my grandmother) had forgiven him as well and was now waiting for his arrival in the spirit world. With the little energy he had left, he looked at me and said, "*kisahkitin kwiyask*." In English this best translates to, "I love you very much"; words I had never ever heard coming out of his mouth.

If you could just imagine the emotion I felt. I cried hard, yet silently; not wanting him to see. I made sure my head was held high, just so he couldn't see my tears flow. My heart was so heavy, I just wanted to leave and go cry. But I didn't leave. Instead, I sat there, and comforted the man that had hurt me so much; the man who had hurt so many. I spent three days alone with my father. I didn't call any family members to come sit. I sat alone with him until his last night. I finally called my uncle Les to come sit with us. A few more people dropped in but I was mostly alone with him. It had to be that way. I needed to get a perspective on what I would have to do to unload the burden I had carried for so long. Those three days were filled with me thinking back to those same memories mom and I had shared so many years ago.

One memory I had of my dad was a time when my mom had run away from him. He had beaten her up again, so she left to hide. That time, she didn't take me with her but it wasn't by choice. He had been hitting her and, at some point, brought his gun out. We were outside and I still remember looking down toward the road. My mom was on the ground as he was yelling at her to get up. She got up and started running toward the road as he pointed the gun at her. I was screaming for him to stop, but he still shot. Thankfully, he missed. He took a few more shots, and missed each time. Thank God he was a crappy hunter, because she managed to get away. I don't recall too much after that, but I remember being with him for a few days before he decided to go look for her.

We were walking towards another family's home and it appeared they had been drinking there. My father and I were looking around the house for mom, but she was not there. There was a drunk woman there, asking my dad to go into the sleeping area with her. A door separated the sleeping area and I could see two beds in there. Her husband was in the eating and sitting area, and was clearly passed out. My father told me to sit on the chair beside the passed out man. He told me he was going to speak to the woman alone so he could get information on where my mom might be. I didn't trust either of them, so I pretended to obey and sat quietly. Once they were in the sleeping area, I snuck to the doorway and peeked in through the door opening. I saw my dad. His hand was under the woman's dress and she was moaning. I didn't believe he was beating her, so I stood frozen wondering what he was doing. After his hand came out from under her dress, she reached over and grabbed a bottle of wine to hand to him. Years later, I realized that my dad had pimped himself out for a swig of wine. Gross!

Not all memories of my dad were bad ones. One time, we were out on our boat, going across the lake to meet with the other families that were commercial fishing. We were just approaching the beach when there was a moose swimming along close to the shoreline. My dad dropped my mom and I off and sped off with another man on our boat. They raced to where the moose was and start circling around it. The moose started to tire from not having anywhere to swim so he slowed down the pace. My dad held up an axe and chopped the moose right between the eyes. My father and the other man hauled the moose in as the women waited patiently by the shore, ready to cut the moose up. The campfire that night was full of laughter, heroism, and a cooked moose meal. This was a great memory. It is these memories I grasp at to overpower the others; the memories where happiness lived and a moment when we had peace.

After my dad died, I took his ashes home with me. At first, it was weird having the ashes there. I wasn't scared of the ashes as I found myself talking to them because I still had unresolved issues. I began to obsess with the memories and, one night when I was sleeping, I had the worst nightmare ever. I wasn't feeling well, so I moved to the guest room. I fell asleep immediately and found myself in one of those dreams that seemed real. In my dream, I was sleeping when someone walked into my room. I felt fear. I knew I was about to be sexually violated, but was helpless to move or run. I became frozen and unable to move, and the figure was moving closer and closer to me. I fought to wake up, and when I did, I found myself pushed up against the wall on my bed. I was awake now and had cold beads of sweat dripping down my skin. My heart was racing and I began to cry. At that moment, I realized that I haven't forgiven my father yet. I still have to work harder to find ways to resolve this.

FINDING THE FIRE

I am sharing my story, because I am able to. I am stronger now than I ever have been, and although I still carry some fears with me, I think the conversation is worth the risk. There isn't anything anyone can do to me today that can be worse that what I have survived. The worse part of my story is this story continues, with another child, and another family. My cycle is broken.

I was a victim of sexual assault by a family member. This is such a taboo subject, and what is even more taboo is to discuss incest. I know incest still does exist in our communities, but it is not talked about. There is so much shame in bringing it out by the victims. If these issues are still in our communities, then how can they be addressed in a safe and compassionate manner?

Healing is key. To heal means to walk back to the power of one's culture. Throughout my healing journey, I have hired professional therapists, and psychologists. However, nothing compares to the healing I have found in my ceremony and in the land. I find that too many of us have become so hung up on buying. We buy programs to read, we buy programs for math, and we buy services to heal. This does not feel right for me as an Indigenous person. What is wrong with what I have? What is wrong with my own cultural practices and beliefs that I have to depend on Western systems to help me?

My best healing has come from understanding who I am, as an Indigenous person. I heal because I share, and I share because I heal. As a Cree woman, I draw on my ancestral strength. I remember the first few visits back to Molanosa, our old home site. My wounded spirit was drawn to the land, and although there were many bad memories surrounding me, I felt the strength of my grandmothers. It was the grandmothers that sent the eagle to watch over us that day. The eagle was telling me that I was going to be okay. The eagle was also telling me that the healing powers of my ancestors cannot be found in a book, cannot be packaged in a box, nor can they be found in a Western clinic. The eagle told me that healing could be natural and holistic.

In November, 2016, I was a keynote speaker at a Youth Empowerment gathering in La Ronge, Saskatchewan. During my presentation, I had a group of volunteers come up to wear my labels. One youth volunteer wore "Sexual Abuse", another wore "Violence in the home". I had others wear, "Child Neglect," "Physical Abuse," and so on. I had a total of twelve youth wearing my labels, while many parents and other youth watched. I went on to talk about how I thought I may have overcome these. I talked to them about our fire within. We all have one. Sometimes our fire becomes so weak that we might think it doesn't exist anymore. But it does! It is there, buried deep within, waiting for us to rekindle and reignite it. Like any fire that has been reduced to an ember, it does take work to build up the flame again. As long as we believe that, that tiny, little spark will never die; we can have hope. I went on to tell that group that all we need is for one person to start the journey to heal… then another, and another… and another. Together we can draw on one another's strength.

When I think back to how or why I overcame so much, there were many factors that definitely came into play. Before everything else, I was blessed to have had a community of mothers: late Jean Beatty, late Ruth Nelson, late Caroline Nelson, late Clara Nelson, my Aunt Mildred, my Aunt Nancy, my sister, late Margaret Brown, and my mom, late Jean Brown. All these incredible women played a role in shaping me, in keeping my fire alive. When my mom quit drinking, even though I was already a rebellious teen, it still made a huge impact in my life. She understood the urgency of giving me life lessons that, I am sure at times, she wondered if any would have stuck with me. I get a sense of fulfilment knowing that I am trying my best to live life in a good way;

in a way that she would be proud of me. All these women gave me homes, meals, and kind words of guidance.

I believe that my determination and strong spirit played a role in guiding me to where I am now. I remember overhearing a conversation amongst two teachers that went something like this: "Poor Nancy, she doesn't have a chance." I never forgot those words and, in fact, I made it my motto, *Tell me I can't and I will*. I am sure there were other teachers that felt the same way as those two who didn't believe I could. I am sure I was just a name on the Register; a ghost passing through their classrooms. Many did not have to tell me; they showed me. Then, there were those few, literally a handful that poured hope into my dream bucket. I always worked hard for them. I had to. They expected great things of me. For every label I wore, I found a way to turn it around; even if all it meant was doing the opposite.

I think about Anna, Jasmine, Patty, Wendy and Stella. These women live among us. They are not ghosts. They are our mothers, sisters, daughters, aunts, cousins and friends. I think about society's treatment of Indigenous people and, more so, Indigenous women. They are the carriers of life, the carriers of song, story, and dance. At any moment, my life could have turned worse, and still now today, I don't take anything for granted. If I am given one more sunrise or one more sunset, I am happy.

I don't know if my soul will ever be truly settled, but maybe I don't want it to be. Maybe the unsettling is what keeps my fire going. Maybe it is what motivates me to keep fighting for those who cannot fight for themselves. Maybe it is what gives voice to those who are silent. Maybe it is what keeps me on my journey to finding lost.

Jamie

I love you, and I write this book for you. Read this and know that I worked hard to break the many cycles that have hurt me. You gave me reason to do this. You were my first-born. Whenever I looked into your eyes, I knew that life was worth living; that I had to trudge on to give you something better. I am proud of all your accomplishments and for all that you challenge yourself to do.

Criss

I love you, and I write this book for you. Read this and know that I value the journey that you and I have gone on during the writing of this. When I look at you, I see wisdom beyond your youth. I am so proud of you. You are creative, generous and smart. You have so much to offer the world. You have given me the greatest gift, my grandchild, and I will forever feel blessed.

Glenn

I love you, and I write this book because of you. I find strength in the love you give me. For every tear that has fallen from my eyes, you have replaced it with smiles, with memories, and with love and laugher. I am proud to walk this journey with you beside me, always ensuring I am safe.

Printed in Canada